THE AUTISTIC GUIDE TO ADVENTURE

THE AUTISTIC GUIDE TO ADVENTURE

Active Pursuits from Archery to Wild Swimming for Tweens and Teens

Allie Mason

Illustrated by Ella Willis

Jessica Kingsley Publishers
London and Philadelphia

First published in Great Britain in 2023 by Jessica Kingsley Publishers
An imprint of Hodder & Stoughton Ltd
An Hachette UK Company

1

Copyright © Allie Mason 2023

Front cover images source: Ella Willis.

A CIP catalogue record for this title is available from the British Library and the Library of Congress

ISBN 978 1 83997 217 1
eISBN 978 1 83997 218 8

Printed and bound in Great Britain by Clays Limited

Jessica Kingsley Publishers' policy is to use papers that are natural, renewable and recyclable products and made from wood grown in sustainable forests. The logging and manufacturing processes are expected to conform to the environmental regulations of the country of origin.

Jessica Kingsley Publishers
Carmelite House
50 Victoria Embankment
London EC4Y 0DZ

www.jkp.com

For Alex – I promise, it gets better.

CONTENTS

ACKNOWLEDGEMENTS

This book would not have been written without the continuous supply of coffee and assorted snacks brought to me by my long-suffering partner, Chris. It's as much his literary child as it is mine, for he carried the burden of caring for our household and dog, Lena, whilst I buried myself in paper and ink. Ich danke dir aus tiefstem Herzen, mein Schatz. And Lena – the emotional support (and excuse to get some fresh air after a mammoth writing session!) has not gone unappreciated. I'm sure a new squeaky toy can be arranged as a token of my gratitude.

To my best friend Leah, I must also give heartfelt thanks, for being the proofreader of my drafts. You didn't even think twice before agreeing to give up your precious summer days, but then, I expected nothing less. You've always been there for me, whenever I have needed you.

It would be remiss of me not to mention as well the invaluable advice I received from fellow JKP author Lydia Wilkins. You were a few steps ahead of me throughout this process and I am so grateful that you shared your wisdom with me along the way. It's simply not possible to quantify the worth of having someone to both commiserate and celebrate with through the rollercoaster journey that is writing a book.

This naturally leads me to Ella, whose drawings have brought life and vivacity to the activities within these pages. Our collaboration has been a joy and I'm excited to see where your talents will take you next. Thank you for illustrating what it means to be autistic and adventurous.

Then, of course, we have my family. They'd never let me get away with not mentioning them here! But how could I not? This book is a culmination not just of the hard work of writing it but also the hard work of getting me, the author, to this point in my life in the first place. Throughout the years my family have been by my side, each offering support in their own way. They've encouraged my storytelling since the very beginning and for that: THANK YOU.

Last, but by no means least, to my contributors, the eclectic selection of fabulous autistic people profiled within these pages, thank you for putting your trust in me to share your story with the world. It was a pleasure to work with you and I do so hope we all stay in touch. You've added an extra wonderful dimension to *The Autistic Guide to Adventure* that I couldn't have pulled off on my own.

MY STORY

Where It All Began

The journey to writing this book began when my brother Josh and I decided to climb Scafell Pike on Christmas Day in 2019. For those of you who are not familiar with Scafell Pike, it is the highest mountain in England, at 978 metres above sea level. A popular tourist attraction for hikers throughout the year, on Christmas Day it was almost deserted, like we had the whole mountain to ourselves. But I'm getting ahead of myself!

We left in the dark, early in the morning, for a two-hour drive from our parents' home in the Yorkshire Dales to the Lake District, where Scafell Pike awaited us. We had Christmas songs on in the car and felt like we were always one bend of the road ahead of the sunrise. I'd made sure to borrow a pair of hiking poles from my grandparents, to help with my balance and spatial awareness. They'd also supplied us with a map and written directions for our ascent, plus a Mars bar each to replenish our energy levels when we reached the summit.

Except we never did.

Did I forget those much-needed hiking poles and leave them on my parents' porch? Yes, yes I did. Was it a mistake for me to be in charge of directions, leading us to climb the nearby Illgill Head instead? Yes, yes it was. Yet despite these 'failings', that Christmas Day hike remains a treasured memory, the first spark of the fire that fuels my aspirations to this day.

Plus, the view of Scafell Pike from the summit of Illgill Head was pretty spectacular.

Being Autistic

Several months earlier in 2019 I had read an article in *Women's Health* magazine that changed my life. A bold claim, I know, but bear with me. It was written by Hannah Molesworth, a 26-year-old autism awareness campaigner. In her article she talked about being diagnosed with anxiety and depression in her teenage years, after struggling with interpersonal relationships and overwhelming emotional responses to social and sensory stimuli. For anyone with an understanding of autism, those traits will be instantly recognizable, yet Hannah didn't receive a formal diagnosis until she was 23. As I read, it became clear that the experiences she was describing could easily have been lifted from my own life.

I, too, had been told by my GP as a teenager that I had anxiety and depression. During my GCSEs and A-Levels I missed months of schooling because I was incapable of leaving my own house. With hindsight it's evident that I had reached a point of shutdown, which is when an autistic individual is so overwhelmed by their senses, emotions and/or social surroundings that they can only maintain their most basic functions. Even then, tasks such as communicating or eating can become insurmountable obstacles.

After reading Hannah's article, I knew that I wanted to confirm if I really was autistic, as I now suspected. Initially, I began by researching preventative coping mechanisms to avoid shutdown and implemented them in my daily life. A few months passed and I could see the positive impact that these changes were having on my wellbeing, so I decided to go to another GP and ask to be referred for a formal assessment. I was incredibly fortunate and was seen within six months of that referral by the assessment team. Depending on where you live (either within the UK or another country), that wait can take years.

At 23 – coincidentally, the same age as Hannah Molesworth – I was diagnosed with Autistic Spectrum Condition. This was a pivotal moment that led to the final silencing of the little voice inside my head that had spent two decades insisting there was something wrong with me. In fact, it turned out that my brain is just wired differently to most other people's, meaning that I operate within the world in a different way. I used to think that everyone else was simply better at coping with life than me! Now that I have the words to communicate precisely why something is a challenge or barrier for me, it has made a huge difference.

My Little Brother

Now, growing up, the person I always compared myself with the most was my younger brother. There is, of course, an element of proximity to that: I lived with him, spoke to him every day, saw his life unfold first-hand. We shared a lot of experiences, but I feel like we had very different childhoods. Yes, we were raised in the same place, and by the same people, but our personalities couldn't be more different. He was laid-back and I was angsty; he seemed confident and brave when I was mostly anxious and scared. Josh approached new things as if they were a challenge set to test him whilst I ran away from them because they were an opportunity for failure. (It turns out that failing is just discovering a way to do something that doesn't work, giving you a greater chance of doing it the right way the next time – but I didn't learn that until I was an adult!) His mantra was 'when the going gets tough, the tough get going'. When things were tough in my life, I'd hide under my duvet and cry. A lot of you can probably relate to that.

So, our paths ran parallel to one another for many years, with Josh out exploring the world whilst my head was firmly between the pages of a book. Now there's absolutely nothing wrong with that, if that is where you want your head to be. However, I'd listen to my brother's tree climbing, river swimming, wild camping, mountain skiing, marathon cycling tales of adventure, and wish it was me. It wasn't for lack of trying but more that I could never find a way to enjoy those activities without feeling stressed and overwhelmed.

Adventures and Sport

So what did I try as a child? These are the activities I can remember: roller skating, horse riding, ice skating, cycling, hiking, swimming, running, kayaking, canoeing, football, netball, climbing. I was also in the Scouts for a little while, where I'm sure I'll have taken part in other things that I now can't recall. Yet, as I mentioned earlier, these were activities that I desperately wanted to enjoy but that mostly felt pretty dreadful to take part in at the time. With the exception of roller skating, horse riding and ice skating, that is! I'm not able to describe it, but skating rarely causes me any sensory issues, so that's probably why it's still my favourite way to stay fit today. Horse riding also didn't negatively affect me too much, which I think was down to the fact it was a special interest for me then.

It was therefore much safer for me to do my adventuring alongside fictional characters instead. I travelled through Middle Earth with Bilbo Baggins, explored Kirrin Island with the Famous Five and snuck out from St Clare's at night with Carlotta Brown. I loved characters who were brave and fierce, which, to be honest, are still two words that I wish came to mind when people think of me. I know that they are not, because when I asked my partner how he would describe me, he called me a 'Germknödel'. For reference, that's a German dessert consisting of a sweet and fluffy dumpling, normally served drenched in vanilla custard. Somehow, I can't quite picture one of those making it on to the cover of *Outside* magazine.

So there you have it. I was a kid with a dream prevented from making progress towards it by an invisible barrier that I didn't understand. It wasn't until I got my autism diagnosis at 23 that I realized my difficulties in accessing sport and other adventures were down to sensory sensitivities, emotional dysregulation, executive dysfunction and social interaction issues.

Why Me?

Now that you know my backstory, the path to me deciding to write this book has hopefully become clear. It's very much a natural progression of events, wanting to share what I have learned along the way. This subject is understandably very close to my heart, so it seemed fitting that I should be the one to discuss it at length with the world! The 'why' that keeps me going, that has helped power me through stressful days and writer's block, is that the adventure and sport communities need to become more accessible, so that no young person feels prevented from getting involved by fear, misconceptions or lack of confidence. I feel like there is a lot of lost time for me to make up, those childhood years when I missed out on enjoying active pursuits because I had to spend so much time figuring out how to even tolerate them. My childhood self is exactly the person who needed to read this book, so I'm creating the resource that I never had.

I do appreciate, however, that my own lived experience can never be universal. That's why a lot of research has gone into the information included within these pages. What is more, I've also reached out to other autistic people about their relationships with sport and adventure. Throughout these pages you will hear from Finlay the archer, Ailsa the climber, Stuart the cyclist, Ella the illustrator, Holly the hiker, Amelia the horse rider, Chris the kayaker, Alex the photographer, Ashley the runner, Emily the skateboarder, Alice the skier, Layla the stand up paddleboarder, Cassidy the surfer and Sam the triathlete.

Where It's All Going

So what's next for me, I hear you ask? The delightful truth is that I don't know yet! There are many active pursuits in this book that I haven't had the chance to try yet, so that's always an option. There are others that I've done once or twice when I was younger but would be keen to try again. And, of course, Scafell Pike, the mountain that I didn't quite conquer on a cold Christmas Day in 2019...something tells me that one day, I'll be going back!

There's also this conversation that will need to be continued, about the lack of representation of autistic people in the adventure and sport communities. Now that I've committed to sharing my thoughts on this subject so publicly, I have a responsibility to keep talking about it. That's the way to ensure that the message keeps reaching more and more of you. Maybe I'll meet you on my next mountain, paddle past you on a kayak trip or wave to you as we comb the beach for treasure. Just remember this: change may be harder for us, but it is not impossible. If, like me, the change you seek is to become more adventurous, I hope this guide helps you to know where and how to start.

HOW TO USE THIS GUIDE

Would this really be an autistic guide if it didn't have a section at the front explaining the different ways you could use it? I think not.

First, let me tell you a bit about how each activity is going to be laid out. They all follow the same structure to begin with: Introduction, Why Try It?, Sensory Expectations, Getting Started! and Support Recommendations. There is then usually a sixth section that covers one of three things: either (1) my first attempt at that activity, (2) information on somewhere in the world that it takes place or (3) a profile of an autistic person who enjoys the activity. There is also an illustration from the lovely Ella for every activity, which is either a drawing of the different kit needed or an artistic impression of someone taking part.

Second, I'd like to recommend three different ways that you can use this book. If you're not sure where to start, you can always just go cover to cover and read through the activities in alphabetical order. If you know that you are interested in a specific type of activity (e.g., land, water, snow, etc.) then you can use the index to find all the ones that fall under that category. If you have the exact activity in mind that you want to try, find it in the contents list and jump straight to it!

I have to note here that some of the activities included in this book can potentially be dangerous if you aren't being supervised or haven't had any training beforehand. That's why it's really important for you to talk to a parent or guardian first, so that they can help you get started in the safest way. There might be skills that you need to work on, such as learning to swim before you take part in any water-based activities, or you might need help finding the right club to join, where you can learn the proper techniques.

Third, you'll notice that there are small coins allocated to each activity. This represents how expensive they are to take part in. One coin = it's low cost, or even free. Two = there's an initial investment required, but after that, you won't need to spend much more. Three = this one will drain your pocket money – and your parents' pocket money, too!

Finally, for 'My Story' (just in case you skipped it already) and 'Allie's Autistic and Adventurous Manifesto', there's no set order that you need to read these in. You can think of them as an introduction and conclusion, or you can dip into them whenever you feel like it. It's totally up to you.

ARCHERY

Introduction

Archery is easily one of the oldest sports that is still practised today, joining running as a recreational activity of the ancient Greeks. As a functional activity, it was a method of war that predates written history. However, as soldiers moved away from the bow and arrow, these became more popular with the middle and upper classes, who began joining archery societies as a hobby from around the 16th century. Since that time archery as a sport has evolved into what we recognize today, first appearing at the Olympic Games in 1900. One of the most interesting things that I learned whilst researching this section is that archery is considered three times safer than golf! Who would have thought that a flying golf ball could pose more danger than an actual arrow...not me!

Why Try It?

So not only is archery a relatively safe hobby, it's been proven to be a relaxing one too. A scientific study has shown that taking part decreases symptoms of stress. This is probably even more true for autistic archers, as the sport is structured around routine and repetition, two things that our brains love! Shooting at a target requires a lot of focus too, meaning that you should find yourself often 'in the zone', where your everyday worries disappear from your mind. Finally, one of the great elements of archery is that you are primarily competing with yourself, to improve the accuracy of your shots or the precision of your technique. You can concentrate on self-improvement without needing to compare yourself to anyone else.

Sensory Expectations

Once upon a time, bows were mostly made from wood, with the accompanying wooden arrows fletched in real birds' feathers! These days, the bow is likely to be made up of multiple materials including laminated wood, plastic and fibreglass, with a nylon bowstring. When you first hold a bow, it would be worth taking the time to get used to the different textures, as well as how you have to position your body to use it. There are lots of smaller items that make up an archer's kit, such as a quiver for arrows, a finger protector and a bracer (to shield your forearm from the released bowstring). It might feel uncomfortable at first to have all these different places of pressure on your body, but this should begin to feel more familiar over time.

Bracer: silicon, rubber or leather with nylon straps

Finger protector: woven fabric or leather with nylon-coated fingertips

Chestguard: woven fabric with plastic and Velcro straps

Getting Started!

It's a good idea to try and find a taster session or beginner course if you like the sound of archery, because it is an expensive hobby.

That way you're not committing too much time and money without knowing whether you enjoy it or not yet! Most clubs will have a minimum joining age, so you'll need to check, before you sign up for anything, that you are old enough. As well as at a club, the other places that you might be able to try out archery for the first time are on school trips to activity centres or on a family holiday to somewhere with organized activities on site.

Support Recommendations

This is likely to be a sport that involves having a coach, to guide you through the journey of improving your technique as an archer. For that reason, it's useful to know what you can ask a coach, to help you thrive during training sessions. For us as autistic folk, it's always best for a coach to focus on what we do need to do (and not distract or confuse us by telling us what not to do!). You could also ask that each session has the exact same structure every time, so that you know what's going to happen and feel more confident. It's worth exploring as well whether you prefer to shoot indoors or outdoors, as then your coach can make sure you always start in the right environment.

PROFILE

Name: Finlay Clark
Country: England
Activity: Archery

How did you first get started with archery?
In the past I had tried many different sports and hobbies. None of

Photo credit: Archery GB and Malcolm Rees

them really worked for me, as they all presented with different small issues that affected my autism. I tried judo as my dad had been competing in this for a long time, but the texture of the floor mats was very sensitive on my skin. My mum's friend's son took up archery and they thought it might suit me, so we went along to a club for a beginners' course and I loved it. This was just before my 10th birthday. Dad and I enjoyed this as our 'dad and son' time.

What are the benefits that you have found from participating in archery?

The benefits in archery for me include meeting and making many friends who accept me for who I am. I don't feel excluded and everyone is friendly. I have managed to be quite successful and now compete at a high level, shooting for Team GB. I enjoy the physical aspect of the sport and have a personal coach. Archery GB provides strength and conditioning coaches and therapists who work with me. I have a training plan that I follow at home and in the gym. I love the routine and repetitive nature of archery, as it really helps me control my emotions.

What are the main sensory issues, if any, that you face whilst participating in archery?

Although there are many aspects of archery that work for me, there have been a few issues that I have had to work through. At times it was really difficult for me, but as I have gotten older, we have developed mechanisms to cope in stressful situations. Initially loud noise would affect me, as clubs use either whistles or beeps to indicate start and stop shooting, so I ask clubs to not blow the whistle too close to me or to place the speakers away from me.

In August 2021 I shot at the European Youth Cup in Romania. The spectators for the teams from other countries were very loud in cheering for their archers. When it was my turn to compete against an Italian archer, one of the judges asked the Italian coach if the team would not cheer as loud during the match, which they did respect. Another issue that used to be problematic for me was shooting in the rain. I couldn't focus when it was raining, which really affected me, and occasionally I had a meltdown at a competition. With help from my coach and parents, I now have coping mechanisms to help in this situation.

How has being autistic impacted you (positively and/or negatively) in this activity?

I think being autistic in archery has mainly had a positive impact for me. As I mentioned before, it is very routine-based, which helps me immensely. I have met many people who may not understand autism but who have always treated me with respect and compassion. I also think that in some way I am educating them, because many people don't know how to speak to someone with autism. I may have a few quirks (that is what my mum calls them!) that people find odd, but once they get to know me, they accept me. Another positive for me is that I don't tend to get nervous at competitions, which may be a big advantage over other archers.

What advice would you give to an autistic young person who is interested in starting archery?

For most clubs in the UK, the minimum age to start archery is around 10 years old, but check this with your local club. You can find clubs on the website of your national archery organization, such as Archery GB in the UK. When you go along to a club, speak to them about your specific needs because they will be inclusive. Clubs run beginners' courses throughout the year, and some even do 'taster/have a go' sessions. Most importantly, enjoy yourself, have fun and don't be scared to have a go!

BEACHCOMBING

Introduction

Beachcombing is an activity that can serve many different purposes, from helping scientists to study tidal patterns and marine biodiversity, to captivating those who seek washed-up treasures as a hobby. Historically, beachcombing was a way for locals to gather natural resources provided by the sea. In some parts of the world today this is still the custom, with children being sent to find items in the sand that could be sold on for profit, adding to their family income. For hobbyists, however, the lure of this activity is the

chance to grow their trove of treasures. Some beachcombers are very particular about what they collect. On the Cornish coast in England, for example, the prize to find is a piece of LEGO®; these continue to be washed up to this day after a full shipping container fell into the sea on its way by cargo ship to New York City in 1997!

Why Try It?

The sheer variety of potential things to be found is what makes beachcombing such an exciting pastime. Sea glass, historical artefacts, shark teeth, shards of pottery, bones, fossils, seashells and more could all be left behind by the receding tide for you to discover. Want to experience a real sense of achievement? Why not decide on the type of item that you would like to collect and then plan your trips around trying to find the more unusual things on your wish list? With planning and research required beforehand, dedication and a keen eye for detail needed on the day, as well as the chance afterwards to turn your treasure into jewellery, crafts or home decor, beachcombing is a surprisingly stimulating hobby.

Sensory Expectations

Sensory seekers are likely to love getting involved with this activity. The smell and taste of salt in the air, the sunlight reflecting off the ocean, the rolling waves in their ears... There are few places better than the beach with its breadth of sensory input. That's without even mentioning the colours and textures of all the different items hidden in the sand. Sea glass, for instance, comes in every hue, from purple to green to gold and anything in-between. Shells are common in a range of shapes and textures: conical, oval, slender, smooth, whorled, ridged, rough, flat, concave. However, from my experience, the most important thing to remember when visiting the beach is that sand invades every piece of your clothing. If, like me, the sensation of grains of sand against your skin is enough to make you want to scream, you should definitely stick to beachcombing on pebbled shores only.

Getting Started!

There are two different ways to take up beachcombing as a hobby. The first is to take your treasures home with you at the end of the day. The second is to 'photo hunt', which means taking a picture to document what you have found and then leaving it there when you go. It should be noted that this second way of beachcombing is the only one allowed in national parks and other protected landscapes. It is also essential to adhere to the rule that you should never kill, harm or take a living creature, which includes ensuring that you leave behind anything that could be the home of, or food for, a living creature. If you follow this rule, all you have to worry about is choosing a beach to visit and packing enough snacks to get you through the day!

Support Recommendations

So that you get the most out of your beachcombing experience, it is best to be prepared and to be safe. In the first instance, take some kind of identification guide with you for whatever it is that you decide to start collecting. This could be a deck of shell cards, a sea glass colour chart or a handbook of marine artefacts. If you prefer to carry information digitally, there is a huge array of websites, blogs and apps available to you on this topic online. In the second instance, be aware of the hazards around you on the beach, such as slippery wet rocks or gradually eroding cliffs. Should you be the kind of person who becomes hyperfocused on their activities to the extent that you forget the rest of the world exists (this is where I raise my hand!), then it would be sensible to have a beachcombing buddy with you to ensure you don't trip face-first into a rock pool.

ALLIE'S FIRST ATTEMPT

Ever since I was a child I've been a beachcomber without even realizing it. As I don't enjoy swimming or playing in the sea, I've always gravitated towards collecting pretty rocks and shells instead. Sometimes I join in on the sandcastle building (with a bucket and spade to avoid touching the sand!), but mostly I can be found searching the shore for new colours of pebbles to add to my collection. This is always done with trepidation because I am terrified of accidentally coming across a crab. The way that they scuttle gives me the jitters.

At the time of writing, I have 11 pebbles and 1 tiny shell (the size of my thumbnail!) in my current collection. I'm very selective about shape when I choose which ones to bring home, because they have to fit comfortably in my palm and have no rough edges. My very favourite pebble is a swirly mix of grey, white and pink that I found on a beach on the south coast of Wales.

BMX

Introduction

BMX was born in the early 1970s, when kids began to use motocross dirt tracks for racing one another on their bicycles. Manufacturers soon realized that there was a market for smaller and lighter models because of this, which led to the development of the BMX bike as we know it today. There are two ways to participate in this sport: racing and freestyle. As you can probably guess what the first involves from the name, I'll only explain the second. Freestyle BMX is when riders perform tricks whilst on the ground or in the air, usually on the streets or at skate parks. The first BMX World Championship was held in 1982, with the debut of BMX at the Olympics following much later, in 2008.

Why Try It?

You might not have realized it, but being a BMX rider actually supports you more in building muscle than being a road cyclist, although both sports provide further health benefits such as reducing stress and improving sleep quality. Regardless of whether you choose to get involved with racing or freestyle, you will see improvements in your coordination, strength and balance. Plus, BMX is a great way to incorporate exercise into your weekly routine on your own terms. There's no membership like at a gym or club; you can just grab your BMX bike and head outside whenever you feel like it.

Sensory Expectations

Sensory seekers, this one is for you! Riding a BMX stimulates your vestibular system (the one responsible for balance) through its changes of direction and speed. Your body will experience resistance and impact through the handling of the bike, especially for freestylers. A BMX bike is designed specifically so that it is light enough to manoeuvre on or around almost anything! The thick wheels exist to offer some cushioning against impact, whilst the handlebars are designed to be easy to spin (often without brakes, to enable the full 360 degrees).

BMX gloves: woven fabric with foam palm reinforcement, insulated lining and elasticated cuffs

BMX helmet: plastic shell with foam padding

Protective pads: elastic and Velcro straps, plastic shell and foam padding

Getting Started!

You can choose to buy the kit that you need for this sport new or second hand, whether that be online or at a local cycling shop. Maybe one of your friends or relatives already has a BMX bike that you could ask to borrow and try out for yourself! In addition to the actual bike, you should wear a helmet and a set of protective pads to keep you safe. To get started with learning, you have a number of options. Have a go and figure it out along the way; ask an experienced friend or relative to teach you; watch some video tutorials online; or, head down to your local skate park and ask the friendly neighbourhood kid to show you what they know. One top tip before you ride anywhere is, if your BMX bike doesn't have brakes, you will have to use the sole of your shoe pressed against the back tyre to slow down and/or stop.

Support Recommendations

If you decide to pursue freestyle BMX, it's worth thinking about how you would feel spending time at a skate park where there are likely to be lots of other riders. If socializing is not your thing, consider planning your practice sessions for quieter times in the day or giving racing another chance (as this generally doesn't involve quite as much social interaction). If being a freestyler at the skate park is the route for you, keep in mind that wooden ramps and obstacles absorb more of your impact whilst performing tricks than their concrete counterparts. Always respect your own sensory limits: if you begin to feel like you're not having fun anymore, it's okay to go home and come back another time.

WHERE IN THE WORLD?

In the Colombian rainforest of South America, on the outskirts of the city of Buga, you can find a house with a difference. It is where BMX freestylers and identical twins Queensaray and Lizsurley Villegas live with their parents. What makes their house so special is that on its roof is a foam-filled pit built from old tyres, mattresses and scrap pieces of wood. When the twins first started their BMX careers in 2016, their family couldn't afford to buy the proper protective equipment for them. So instead, their father built the pit on top of their house with materials he could source from the local community. There is a ramp leading to it from the rainforest, allowing Queensaray and Lizsurley to practise their BMX tricks without fear of injury. If you search for their names online, you can see this amazing construction for yourself in a short documentary about the sisters, made by Red Bull.

CAMPING

Introduction

For most of human
history, camping was
solely a necessary
activity that took place
on a journey from one
location to another. That
began to change in the
late 19th and early 20th

centuries, when camping for the fun of it became a fashionable
pastime. In the USA, this was popularized through the writings
of John Muir, a generously bearded naturalist who lived in a one-
roomed wooden cabin that he had built himself, in what would
eventually be known as Yosemite National Park. Many of these
early recreational campers chose to travel and subsequently stay
in relative luxury, with a comfortable train journey delivering them
to their fully furnished tents. Others would hire a team of mules
to carry their substantial collection of camping equipment (later
replaced by an automobile when these became more widely driven).
I like to think that this might have been where the phrase 'packing
everything but the kitchen sink' originated. It certainly seems like
these campers were taking as much of their daily household items
with them as they could!

Why Try It?

You could probably write a whole book in and of itself about
why a person should consider going camping for the first time.

In my research for this section, however, I came across three interconnected reasons to have a go that I thought were especially compelling. Let me share them with you now:

1. Our 21st-century lifestyles are full of stress, even as teenagers. Yet there is significant research to prove that just being outside in the natural world is enough to reduce stress – what's not to love about that? So that means camping in nature could be a great way for you to feel calmer and less anxious.

2. You've probably heard of your circadian rhythm before now, which is the system in your body that regulates important processes like sleep and digestion. Camping is one method of resetting your circadian rhythm to match the natural rising and setting of the sun, which, in turn, could improve the functioning of those important processes.

3. As autistics we often struggle with our memories, paying attention and the ability to regulate our emotions – but did you know, these are all things that can be negatively affected by regularly using your smartphone? Getting out to camp in a remote area without any phone signal would give you a break from your digital devices and hopefully put less pressure on your memory, attention span and emotions for a while.

Sensory Expectations

The aspect of camping that I find most challenging from a sensory perspective is that I am forced to complete familiar everyday routines in an unfamiliar environment. What you are able to cook and eat is limited by the equipment that is available, so anything that relies on an oven or microwave – as an example – is out of the question. You can often find alternative ways to cook certain foods, but this will change the texture and taste. What you wear to sleep and the bedding that you sleep on will need to differ from what you are used to at home, as the temperature is likely to be colder in a tent at night (depending on where in the world you live). Plus, being outside means that there aren't four walls dampening the noises around you. Be prepared to hear the sounds of the elements and wildlife as you're falling asleep, unless you bring ear plugs. Another option is to stay in a caravan rather than a tent, which would be a more similar experience to staying at home, while still exploring the great outdoors.

Getting Started!

Earlier I mentioned the American John Muir, who has a British counterpart in Thomas Hiram Holding. THH, as we'll now call him, was seen as a pioneer of recreational camping in the early 20th century. He even wrote *The Camper's Handbook*, which is all about how to start camping for the fun of it. It's sadly quite difficult to get your hands on a copy today, so here are a few things that THH recommends considering when you are planning your first trip:

- Setting up camp: Where do you want to go and what terrain will that involve?
- Types of tent: How many people will your tent need to sleep, and will the weather conditions be good enough for you to maybe use a quick-pitch/instant model for ease?
- Food: How many meals do you need to pack for, and in which ways could you incorporate safe foods (with tastes, smells and textures that you enjoy) into your menu?
- Clothes: What will the weather be like during your trip (as this will dictate the clothes that you'll need), and do you have enough layers for the cold nights (if applicable)?
- Equipment: How will you carry all of your camping gear, and is there anything that you could manage without to lighten the load?

Support Recommendations

I asked my lovely Instagram followers to share their best advice for going camping when you are autistic. Here is what they had to say:

- Take lots of blankets to sleep on top of, so that you aren't kept awake by the feeling of rocky ground beneath your body.
- Get a slightly bigger tent than you think you will need, as then you can freely move around and avoid feelings of claustrophobia.
- Pack safe food snacks, so that if cooking your main meal goes wrong, you have backup food options to prevent you from going hungry!

ALLIE'S FIRST ATTEMPT

Growing up, camping was a regular part of my year because my parents were both leaders in the Scouts and Guides. That meant that from the age of 2½ I was tagging along on all of their trips! At that young age I would be carried around on someone's back in a child rucksack, which, to be honest, looks like it was a lot of fun. I asked my parents what I was like as a toddler on these camping trips, and the stories that they shared came as no surprise in light of my late diagnosis as autistic. Apparently, I hated the touch of grass on my skin so much that they could safely leave me on a blanket by the tent whilst they got on with other jobs, knowing that I wouldn't move off it for fear of coming into contact with the 'green stuff'. Also, if we ever visited the beach during a trip and they tried to put me down on the sand, I would scream and scream until someone picked me up again.

CANOEING

Introduction

The canoe first came into being as a method of travel for the native tribes of America, later to be adopted and eventually made recreational by European colonizers. In those early days a canoe would have been built from the wood of trees growing near the waterways that the Native Americans used. It was then, and remains to this day, an open-top boat powered by a single bladed paddle. After the American Civil War, recreational canoeing became a popular way for two young people to spend time together without a chaperone (see also the section on roller skating). Whilst retaining the same basic design, modern canoes are now made from materials such as plastic or fibreglass.

Why Try It?

Arguably, one of the most exciting elements of travelling along a waterway in a canoe is that the wildlife there is more curious around paddlers, for the most part. This means you may get lucky and see animals that are often out of sight for the average passer-by! Whilst watching the wildlife you'll also be getting a good workout, as canoeing relies on the majority of the muscles in your arms and shoulders. For that reason, too, it's a great activity to have a go at for anyone with a lower body impairment. As with many of the active pursuits within these pages, the combination of exercise in connection to the natural world through canoeing can contribute to better mood, lower stress levels and improved sleep quality.

Sensory Expectations

From my own experience, the water on which you are canoeing will yield the larger part of the sensory input that you encounter. Sunlight on a bright day reflects off the surface and produces glare, whilst the motion of the boat can either arouse or calm your sense of balance. If canoeing along the coast, the smell and taste of salt can take some adjusting to. Then there is the kit that you will need to wear for your safety: a snug-fitting helmet and buoyancy aid. Ensure these are comfortable before leaving the shoreline to avoid any potential niggling distractions once out on the open water.

Helmet: plastic shell, foam padding and nylon strap

Paddle: aluminium shaft with rubber handgrip

Buoyancy aid: nylon outer shell, PVC padding, elasticated sides and nylon straps

Getting Started!

The best place to learn to canoe is at a local club, because they will be able to provide you with every piece of specialized kit and equipment that you need. All you would have to do is turn up in clothes and shoes that you don't mind getting wet. Most clubs will run free or low-cost taster sessions for anyone interested in exploring whether canoeing might be the right hobby for them. Otherwise, an alternative option to have a go would be to hire a canoe with family and/or friends for a few hours on a local waterway. You might start out paddling around in circles until you get the hang of it, but at least you'll all be having fun at the same time!

Support Recommendations

As I mentioned earlier, canoeing is a very accessible sport for those with lower body impairments, so if that is relevant to you or one of your paddling companions, make sure to find a club or provider that has adaptive seating for mobility aid users. It's also an accessible activity to those with visual or auditory impairments if the instructor uses a radio for communication between boats (connected to an earpiece or hearing aid in the latter case).

ALLIE'S FIRST ATTEMPT

As a member of the Scouts, I tried a number of different water sports, including canoeing. There was a lake that we used to go to as a troop where I once left my waterproof trousers. My mum was not best pleased when I came home without them! I remember how uncomfortable the buoyancy aids were that we had to wear, with the straps distractingly scratching my chin throughout our time on the lake. I've never been the biggest fan of being in water – I love the sound of it, and I love watching it, but going from dry skin/clothes to wet skin/clothes is a real sensory challenge for me. So you can imagine that canoeing with a group of teenage boys intent on splashing each other with their paddles wasn't the greatest experience. Having said that, I recently went canoeing again as an adult and had the most wonderful time. The rhythm of paddling and the resistance of the paddle as it pushed against the water was so soothing for me.

CLIMBING

Introduction

Back in ancient times our ancestors would have primarily climbed out of necessity, to escape threats such as hungry wild animals or enemy tribes. Since then, climbing has become a recreational activity, something that people do for the enjoyment and thrill of it. This shift in the way that society views climbing came about in the late 19th century, with the mid-20th century seeing the first recorded exploits of recreational climbers using the facades of buildings as a place to practise their skills. Indoor climbing rose in popularity after the first purpose-built walls were constructed in the 1980s. With both outdoor and indoor options this sport has proven to be very accessible to those who use mobility aids as well. For example, in 2012 a team of three paraclimbers completed the first all-disabled ascent of El Capitan in Yosemite National Park, a 1000-metre vertical rock formation that is world-renowned for its difficulty.

Why Try It?

In addition to being an accessible activity for mobility aid users, rock climbing is well suited to the workings of our autistic minds. It is an activity that rewards problem-solving and hyperfocus, as climbers seek to assess the best method for reaching the summit. Plus, practising challenging movements and sequences over and over again until perfected appeals to our preference for repetition and routine. This activity also provides an opportunity for social interactions in a structured setting, as every climber will have somebody else belaying for them. Belaying is when a second person pulls a rope through a mechanical device called a belay, which acts as a brake to stop the climber falling if they slip. Taking on this key supporting role gives a satisfying sense of responsibility and a mutual feeling of achievement when the climber reaches the top of the wall or rock formation.

Sensory Expectations

There is likely to be a lot of sensory input involved in this activity, whether that be on an indoor wall or an outdoor rock face. This is because it is essential for the person climbing and the person belaying to be in communication at all times, which can naturally lead to a lot of shouting! There will usually be multiple people

Chalk bag: polyester outer shell, fleece lining and elasticated drawstring

Climbing harness: woven fabric with mesh padding and nylon straps

Helmet: plastic shell, foam padding and nylon strap

Climbing shoes: knitted upper with Velcro straps and rubber sole

attempting the same ascent simultaneously (unless specifically requested otherwise), which can present not only an auditory but also visual distraction. If you are climbing outside rather than on an indoor wall, you'll need to think about how the weather and the temperature might affect you as well. For both locations, if you are climbing at height you will need to wear a safety harness, which some could find uncomfortable when it presses into the lower body. Having said all of that, autistic rock climbers report that being in a state of hyperfocus on the moves and sequences does mitigate against these inputs. As this is such a tactile sport that relies primarily on balance and feeling for holds, it's possible for positive sensory input to be achieved.

Getting Started!

The best way for you to get started with this activity is to try indoor climbing first, before progressing to outdoor climbing once you begin to feel more confident. At an indoor wall, there will be set routes that you can follow as a beginner with guidance from an instructor, without the added pressure of contesting with the outdoor elements. For your first climb, you'll want to wear stretchy clothes that fully cover your arms and legs (because grazes can be painful!). You need to make sure, however, that any top or jacket that you wear doesn't cover your hands. For shoes, the ideal option is to ask at the reception desk if they have any climbing shoes that you can borrow – but just remember to bring your own socks with you! If they don't, hard-soled trainers are the next best thing, so that you can get good purchase with your feet as you ascend. If you find that you can't stand the sensation of the safety harness, there's no need to despair – often climbing centres will also offer bouldering, which takes place at lower heights and therefore doesn't require you to wear a harness.

Support Recommendations

Fortunately, there are many ways that you can be supported to thrive in this new hobby that you have chosen to try. It's always worth asking an instructor in advance of your first few sessions if it would be possible to have nobody else using the same wall as you, to minimize potential distractions. It's also beneficial to ask for either a visual timetable or at least a clear structure of what to expect during the session itself. If requested, it should be easy for the instructor to adapt their session plan so that it focuses on achieving a set goal or on improving a particular skill. Finally, it might be an option to use radios to communicate rather than shouting up and down the wall, as one of the radios can be attached to the harness of the climber and the other can be kept by the instructor. Often these can be set up to directly output to T-loop compatible hearing aids or earpieces if needed.

PROFILE

Name: Ailsa Graham
Country: England
Activity: Climbing

How did you first get started with climbing?

I first started climbing when I was nine years old. I got given a block of six weeks of climbing lessons as my ninth birthday present at my local climbing wall. I loved it so much that I didn't stop. I was much older when I got into outdoor climbing. I did a little bit with my club as a teenager, but didn't get properly into it until my 20s.

What are the benefits that you have found from climbing?

It's a great way to get fit and strong, but more than that, climbing has a fantastic and very open community. It is from climbing that I have made my best lifelong friends.

I have never felt odd or weird when I am with climbers, and for me, that has been the biggest benefit.

What are the main sensory issues, if any, that you face whilst climbing?
I've normally been okay when it comes to my sensory experience. You get used to the feel of the holds, and I have always preferred to wear tighter footwear!

How has being autistic impacted you (positively and/or negatively) in this activity?
It has made me really determined and single-minded with my climbing, which has been both good and bad. I think if I wasn't autistic I might have handled my injury as a teenager better. However, climbing is about problem-solving and thinking, which are both things that I am good at. This sport also needs you to be totally focused on the climb, and being autistic is helpful for that.

What advice would you give to an autistic young person who is interested in starting climbing?
Give it a go! Indoor climbing walls are a great place to start. They often have kids clubs that are in small groups, which I have always preferred. Climbing is a very open and inclusive sport. Some indoor climbing walls may also have programmes or sessions where they take people climbing outdoors too!

CONSERVATION VOLUNTEERING

Introduction

If you are one of the many people today who are worried about the climate crisis, then conservation volunteering could be your way to give back to the planet and have a positive impact on the situation. This activity recognizes the importance of preserving both our natural resources and our wildlife by taking practical action. Our green spaces, from school grounds to local parks to nature reserves, need caring for in order to prosper. That's where conservation volunteering comes in, an experience that not only makes a difference but also provides a feeling of wellbeing and wonder to those who take part in it.

Why Try It?

That feeling of wellbeing stems from contact with nature, which is known to support good mental health. In fact, all aspects of conservation volunteering – including the exercise involved and the social connection gained – are known to do this. As an inclusive activity, you are likely to get to spend time with others from a range of age groups and backgrounds, whilst all working towards the same goal. This teamworking often results in an improvement of social and leadership skills. Plus, the tasks that you do as a volunteer can deepen your understanding of topics such as risk assessment or first aid. One day these skills might just come in handy when applying for your first job!

Sensory Expectations

It's a good idea to ask in advance if you will be expected to wear specific clothing that is provided for you, or if you can wear whatever you feel comfortable in. We are able to volunteer once a month at my current job, so I have spent time helping on a farm where I need to wear overalls. These can take some getting used to and are sometimes tricky to put on in the first place! As most conservation-related tasks take place outside, you need to be prepared for the weather that is forecast. However, if you know that you struggle with a particular type of weather (rain, snow, extreme heat, wind) and that is what is expected on the day you are due to volunteer, don't feel like you can't reschedule or even just miss that session as long as you let your team leader know. You have to do what is right for you and not force yourself to 'push through'. Finally, remember to discuss any sensitivities that you have to textures or smells with your team leader in advance. That way you can feel comfortable in the knowledge that you won't be asked to do something that triggers these.

Getting Started!

This activity is a great way to get your nature fix for free, as anyone can take part regardless of how much money you have or where you live. Even in cities there will be green spaces that need caring for. You can search online for volunteering teams in your area and choose which one to join based on the types of conservation that they do. (Or maybe your school has a club that helps to look after the grounds?) Some teams will work on habitat management, making sure that the local wildlife has a safe environment to live in. Others will plant trees in an effort to address the global issue of deforestation. Should you ever wish to take a break from these more practical tasks, many teams will also spend time educating the wider public about the climate crisis and conservation, through creating posters and leaflets or hosting talks and events. There really is something for everyone!

Support Recommendations

There are lots of ways that your team leader can help you to get the most out of your volunteering experience. You can ask them to be very clear in their communication by setting specific and realistic tasks for you to complete, in addition to giving you a five-minute warning before it is time to change to another task. It might also be useful if they prepare a visual timetable for you of what will happen during the session, or perhaps help you to write down some notes on your phone (if you have one) that can act as cues on which steps to follow during a task.

WHERE IN THE WORLD?

On 13th April 2013 at the Tunku Abdul Rahman Marine Park in Malaysia, the Guinness World Record was set for the longest underwater clean-up by 139 conservation volunteers. Working in teams, 139 divers spent 168 hours and 39 minutes collecting over 3000 kilograms of waste from the marine landscape. This waste was made up of everything from plastic, glass and ceramics to metal, rubber and cloth. In total, the teams completed 1120 dives to remove these materials. The purpose of this organized volunteering event, which attracted divers from all over the world to participate, was to promote marine conservation and create more awareness around the benefits of ecotourism.

CYCLING

Introduction

If you had wanted to ride a bicycle back when they were first invented, in 1817, you'd have had to kick your feet against the ground to get anywhere, as cranks and pedals weren't added until decades later, in 1863. That was when the bicycle was known as the 'boneshaker', but I'll leave it to your imagination to figure out why! The history of this contraption then takes an interesting turn, with inventors seeking to add stability by considerably increasing the size of the front wheel, creating the penny-farthing. These odd machines reached the height of their mainstream popularity in the 1870s and 1880s, before the safety bicycle was developed in 1885 (which most closely resembles in appearance and functionality what we ride today). It is still possible, though, to get your hands on a penny-farthing. There are even international penny-farthing races, should you be so inclined!

Why Try It?

Many cyclists you speak to will associate this hobby with freedom. On two wheels you can go almost anywhere, improving your endurance and general health as you pedal. If you want to ride with friends or family, that's great. If you decide to ride alone, you can enjoy the solitude with a clear mind and experience the world from a different perspective in your saddle. Some of you may have cycled before when you were younger and be wondering, why try it again? The answer is that a return to cycling can help you to build your confidence, both on and off two wheels. Start small and choose a trail or park free from traffic, before working up to cycling alongside other road users, rather than taking on too much, too soon!

Sensory Expectations

You'll definitely be wearing a helmet and probably also cycling gloves and/or padded shorts as you cruise around on two wheels. You want to make sure that these fit well to avoid sensory distractions, so that you can focus on steering and pedalling and everything else that is involved. The helmet needs to be snug on your head and not move around whilst it's worn. It's also a good idea to wear clothes that cover your arms and legs, because this minimizes the risk of sunburn and protects from minor scratches or grazes if you're cycling through the countryside. The padded shorts are important as they provide a much-needed comfort barrier between you and the saddle, especially on any longer rides.

Helmet: plastic shell, foam padding and nylon strap

Trainers: mesh upper, with laces and rubber sole

Cycle shorts: elastane with foam padding

Getting Started!

Now, if you have never ridden a bike before, it might seem daunting as an older child or young adult to start learning at this point in your life. You don't need to feel that way, however. Apply the same approach as any new learner would and you'll soon be on your way to pedalling through your neighbourhood. You've got to start with getting a feel for the bike and how to balance, which you can do by removing the pedals and lowering the saddle slightly. This replicates the original 1817 experience! Push yourself along with your feet until you feel confident controlling the bike. When you first reintroduce your pedals, go somewhere quiet with no hills and a smooth surface to practise. It's a misconception that grass is the best surface type to learn on; it actually makes it much harder for you to push the pedals as a new learner. Once you've learned control and pedalling, you're ready to move on to a traffic-free environment, like a park.

Support Recommendations

Sometimes we learn best by copying others, so you might like to ask someone you know who can already ride to demonstrate what to do. That person could then walk or jog alongside you as you start out, to help stabilize you until you're confident with using the brakes to stop. When going on rides with friends or family, ask them to let you set a pace and mileage that you are comfortable with. On longer rides, I'd recommend scheduling regular breaks, to fuel up with snacks and check in as to how your energy levels are. Communication is key! If you're tired or starting to feel overwhelmed, it would be dangerous to try and carry on without a break.

PROFILE

Name: Stuart Watson
Country: England
Activity: Cycling (Mountain Biking)

How did you first get started with cycling?
I remember going with my dad to the local bike shop and buying a

second-hand BMX-style bike. It was blue with white tyres. It had stabilizers on at first, but after taking them off, crashing into a gate and grazing myself, then getting straight back on, I was hooked. I definitely recall cycling home from primary school on this bike before I was quite ready for that journey! Fast-forward 30 years...me and my dad were still mountain biking together whenever we could.

What are the benefits that you have found from cycling?
Riding a bike gives you the freedom to travel to places independently. I would ride my dirt jump bike before and after secondary school, whenever it was dry. As soon as the holidays arrived, I would cycle 3.5 miles to the local woods, where there were lots of small hills and roots to make the riding interesting. I loved the feeling of the bike gripping the ground and the pressure of the terrain pushing back up. Or the feeling of weightlessness when you launch off a well-crafted jump. I still enjoy these feelings! I've learned that their scientific names are proprioceptive and vestibular feedback, important for supporting our systems of body awareness and balance.

What are the main sensory issues, if any, that you face whilst cycling?
My main sensory challenges are sound and touch. Luckily, mountain biking is often in woodland areas. The dampening effect from the trees and shrubs makes the sound environment when I'm biking about as ideal as it could be for me. Inside buildings or in urbanized areas with lots of people and/or vehicle traffic, I usually wear noise-cancelling headphones. I'm wearing them right now in my quiet home office. I can hear the shape of the room if I don't wear them! I never had the opportunity to speak to people who understood this until the past year or so when I met the online autistic community. Lauren Melissa Ellzey

in particular helped me to understand so many of my stims through active pursuits like biking and kayaking. Mountain biking gives me the sensory input I need.

How has being autistic impacted you (positively and/or negatively) in this activity?

Scarily, as I look back at many of my outdoor adventures, I realize these are now into their fourth decade! But it's only in the past year I've realized the majority of my anxiety wasn't about the challenges of environment – think big jumps, drops and steep trails – but due to the social challenges that come from riding with other people. Embracing being autistic through a lens of neurodiversity makes it all make sense. I've always been a very cautious rider, but this doesn't stop my progress. I can now ride steep black trails; the scary bit is the small talk at the bottom!

Being autistic means my interest in biking has lasted a very long time. I have routines that I need to navigate the world, which I sometimes struggle to build biking into. However, in those times I can use my brain to visualize trails or feel the feedback from them, without actually riding them. This is something I have finally been able to reflect on and write about since growing my circle of neurodivergent friends, who have helped me to describe my mountain biking experiences in ways I've never had access to before.

Speaking with Allie as part of this book interview process was a great example of how unmasking and just being ourselves whilst talking leads to a deep connection between people. We didn't experience the urge to explain or justify ourselves. Finding people who help you feel like this feels great, just like linking up a new section of trail on your bike.

What advice would you give to an autistic young person who is interested in starting cycling?

Your experiences whilst biking are entirely valid. Notice the pressure to be like other riders, but trust your instincts and let your own unique riding style evolve. Reach out to the autistic community online, as they will be interested to hear more about your adventures!

DRAWING

Introduction

For tens of thousands of years, humans have been communicating through drawing. As a species, we have been drawing pictures for far longer than we have been writing words. The very earliest examples are mainly to be found on cave walls in Spain and France, dating back to a time when woolly mammoths and rhinoceroses roamed the earth. Sadly, I can't guarantee that you'll see either of those for yourself if you go outside to draw today!

Why Try It?

Much like a later pursuit in this book – photography – drawing is an excellent outlet for self-expression. You can draw to communicate, or for cathartic purposes, or even simply to relax. At one level, drawing is brilliant for improving hand–eye coordination and motor skills, which we, as autistic people, sometimes need to work on. At another level, I love the idea that by drawing, you are connecting to an impulse that our ancestors felt all those thousands of years ago. Taking time to draw can benefit you on both a physical and spiritual level – how awesome is that?

Sensory Expectations

As well as the sensory inputs that you'll encounter whilst exploring your local area and beyond, you should also consider the sensory experience of using different materials to draw. Paper can vary in both roughness and thickness, meaning the sound your pen or pencil makes on contact could be scratchy to your ears. Indeed, the paper itself might feel scratchy to your skin, too! If you decide to draw digitally instead, remember that if you are visually sensitive, you might find the backlight of the device you're using could become uncomfortable to your eyes after prolonged periods of looking at it.

Getting Started!

If you have something to draw with or on, whether that be analogue or digital, you have everything that you need to start drawing. You could use a pen or pencil, loose paper sheets or a sketchbook, or a stylus and tablet, if that's what you'd prefer. The only other requirement to begin is to find somewhere or something that you would like to draw. Make like our ancestors and perhaps seek out an animal to be your subject – whilst we haven't got that many woolly mammoths around anymore, there are plenty of other birds, insects, amphibians and mammals to choose from.

Support Recommendations

If you need some inspiration to feel more confident about having a go at drawing, look no further than Instagram. Last time I checked, the hashtag #autisticartist had over 70,000 posts associated with it! It's also good to remember that there is no 'right or wrong' when it comes to drawing. This might sound like an unexpected support recommendation, but being kind to yourself and preparing yourself mentally for the fact that you'll make mistakes, and that that's okay, will go a long way towards helping you to feel less stressed or anxious. I speak from experience!

PROFILE

Name: Ella Willis
Country: England
Activity: Drawing

How did you first get started with drawing?

I have always been really creative, from doodling in my workbooks at school or just constantly having pencils in my hand. I started illustrating digitally during the first lockdown of the pandemic as something to do, and realized it could be a great little business.

What are the benefits that you have found from drawing?

When I feel the urge to draw it's usually because I need some calm or some chill time. I've found that doing it as a business and putting time constraints on myself doesn't work. Illustrating in my own time makes me feel like I have an outlet and a place to retreat to when I need a break.

What are the main sensory issues, if any, that you face whilst drawing?

I used to always be really fussy with paper and pens. I couldn't cope with the rough, scratchy paper; it always had to be of a certain quality. Digital illustration also means that the pen I use on my tablet makes a little tapping noise, which can get very frustrating! But I tend to combine drawing with music or watching TV so I find ways to distract myself.

How has being autistic impacted you (positively and/or negatively) in this activity?

Imagination. I always found that my imagination and my ability to create and think outside of the box was far greater than the people around me. I find that the way I process things and the way that my brain thinks makes it really easy to come up with unique and fun concepts. I used to illustrate characters from books I'd made up to redesigning books I thought could look better, and my parents always used to say how imaginative and uniquely creative I was.

What advice would you give to an autistic young person who is interested in starting drawing?

Put no pressure on yourself and don't feel the need to enter creative spaces and ideas just because someone else is. I would draw things that were considered really strange and felt very self-conscious about the weird characters I would create, but you should never limit yourself to what other people find acceptable. Creative outlets are there for a reason, to be creative in whatever capacity you want.

FISHING

Introduction

With an increased awareness of climate change and interest in being environmentally conscious, thinking about where your food comes from is a natural progression. If you eat fish, have you ever considered trying to catch your own? Fishermen have a responsibility to act as stewards of the lakes and rivers that they travel, catching only what they need and taking care of the waterways that they use. They develop self-reliance through sourcing their own food and a greater appreciation for the circle of life. Oh, and one more thing – if the zombie apocalypse arrives, you can bet they'll still be able to feed themselves!

Why Try It?

You might not have expected it – I certainly didn't – but fishing is a well-suited activity for those of us on the spectrum. It is predictable and repetitive by nature, with a tendency towards smaller groups and pairs that allows for peaceful solitude whilst near the water. Fishing requires concentration for long periods of time, which is a perfect way to channel hyperfocus. It also requires organization, whether that be planning ahead the best spots to visit based on the time of year to ensuring that you have each bit of kit needed to bait your line successfully. All in all, it really plays to our strengths.

Sensory Expectations

What is more, the sensory experience of going fishing has significant potential to be a thoroughly calming one. Most locations such as lakes and rivers have consistent landscapes of muted earthy tones, creating a soothing visual backdrop. As the boats are mostly stationary, there are few aural inputs to irritate beyond the gentle lapping of the water against the hull. Indeed, the light motion of the boat itself is likely to exert a calming effect on your sense of balance. I'm surprised that these fishermen manage to stay awake long enough to catch anything in such a tranquil environment!

Bait: plastic

Rod: fibreglass shaft with foam handgrip

Getting Started!

To begin with, you will need to buy, hire or borrow a fishing rod and some bait, and then decide if you want to fish from a boat or set up on the bank instead. Depending on where you live, you may have to apply for a rod licence (which is free for under-16s in the UK), as well as a permit for the stretch of water that you intend to fish. The latter are usually secured from a local angling club or waterway conservation organization. If you'd like to be taught by an expert rather than teach yourself, these places often offer sessions to help you learn the basics of fishing too. Just remember, different places have different rules as to whether you can keep what you catch or if you must return the fish to the water unharmed, so make sure to check this in advance.

Support Recommendations

When you first start fishing, it is best to avoid setting up on or anchoring near forested banks. This is because you will spend more time trying to free your line from the trees than actually catching any fish! Whether you are teaching yourself or being taught by an expert, learn each task one at a time, making sure that you are comfortable with the stage (baiting, casting, reeling) before moving on to the next one. If you do decide to go out on a boat – accompanied by a parent, guardian or responsible adult – you'd be wise to practise those tasks on land first, as that will give you the best chance of becoming proficient in them before introducing the additional element of the motion of the boat.

WHERE IN THE WORLD?

Across the world, there are many different fishing techniques with ancient origins that our ancestors are known to have used to catch their next meal. Spearfishing, which occurred primarily in shallow waters, was first recorded in India and France 16,000 years ago, but was also a staple hunting method of Native American tribes for over a millennium. Angling, where a hook is attached to a fishing line, can be dated back to the Neolithic age, with the oldest hooks ever discovered being from 22,000 years ago and found in a cave on the Japanese island of Okinawa. Ice fishing is still an essential way of life of the Inuit people of the Arctic and subarctic regions, where a fishing line or spear is used to catch prey through a hole in the frozen surface of a body of water. This is again a hunting method that has been practised for over a millennium.

FORAGING

Introduction

Foraging for food is how our ancestors fed themselves up until the introduction of farming in the late Stone Age. In the 12,000 years since that time, it is a skill that has been lost in many human communities, but not all. There are tribes such as the Hadza in Tanzania who still live off their land, not by domesticating animals or growing fruit and vegetables, but by foraging for edible plants and hunting. This approach to eating connects us with the natural world and compels us to notice how the changing of the seasons impacts what is available. You, too, can learn to forage for edible plants. Which ones to eat and where to look for them will differ, depending on which country you live in and whether your local environment is urban or rural.

Why Try It?

I may be biased (which you'll understand after reading 'Allie's First Attempt' later) but I think foraging is such a lovely way to get back to the nature around where you live. It's an activity that can also be scaled depending on how much time you have and how invested you want to be. There's no expectation that you will be an expert forager the first time that you try. In fact, it's probably best to start small and expand your knowledge over time, focusing on finding and identifying one or two plants to begin with. If you're not keen on the idea of eating the wild foods that you discover, not to worry.

There are many more ways that you can put your new-found foraging skills to good use. Why not collect beautiful flowers to press into a journal, fallen nuts and seeds to craft into home decor, or intricately patterned leaves to serve as drawing inspiration?

Sensory Expectations

Involving more than one of your senses when recognizing different plants is going to make the process much easier, so you can expect to be looking at their appearances as well as smelling their scents and feeling their textures. You should *never*, however, taste a plant if you aren't confident about what it is, because some can be poisonous. Particular scents can often be a trigger for half-forgotten memories. Whenever I smell wild garlic, for instance, I'm always reminded of childhood adventures in the Yorkshire Dales where I grew up.

It's likely that when you are out foraging you'll be visiting the wilder kind of outdoor spaces, with low hanging branches or insects that could scratch at your skin. It is therefore advisable to wear long-sleeved tops and trousers to avoid unpleasant tactile encounters. Tuck those trousers into socks or boots and your sleeves into gloves. The latter is also an excellent method of avoiding the prickles of thorny or spiky plants.

Getting Started!

To begin foraging, your first step is to locate a nearby green space such as a park, field or woodland. Some sites won't be suitable so it's very important to check beforehand if they are protected for conservation, habitats for vulnerable species or facing issues with over-foraging by the public. Normally these types of site will be well signposted and therefore straightforward to avoid. In some local areas there might be experts providing guided tours for beginner foragers to join. Otherwise, you can head out on your own, but just remember to only gather flowers, nuts, seeds, leaves and fruit in the places where they are in abundance. Similarly to beachcombing, it is essential to leave behind enough for animals to eat and plants to regenerate and reproduce from. You don't want to be the reason that a little woodland creature goes hungry!

Support Recommendations

Again, likewise with beachcombing, preparation is key to a successful foraging expedition. It is absolutely necessary to have some kind of identification guide, whether that is a book or a mobile app, which will help you to avoid any poisonous plants. Something like *Foraging with Kids* by Adele Nozedar might be a fun place to start, because in addition to the plant descriptions, there are drawings to colour in and recipes to try with your foraged treasures. There's also no need to worry about straying too far into unknown territory, as it is advised that foragers always stay on the paths, in order to avoid damaging the natural environments that they're collecting from. You can plan your route in advance, safe in the knowledge that there will be no need to deviate from it at any time.

ALLIE'S FIRST ATTEMPT

I genuinely cannot remember a time before I was a forager, because my grandparents have taken me out to pick wild blackberries in the hedgerows from a young age. Here in the UK, August to October is the prime window for blackberry picking. We would bring empty plastic ice cream containers and fill them with berries, before storing them in my grandparents' freezer. Throughout the year my grandma would dip into this fruitful store (no, I couldn't resist the pun) and bake homemade crumbles for the whole family to enjoy with golden yellow custard. I love going blackberry picking because it is such a satisfying pattern hunt – you're looking for berries of just the right colour and size amongst the hedgerow to ensure they are ripe and ready. From my experience, the wild berries are not as sweet as the ones you can buy in the supermarket, so if you don't like sharp tastes, then it would be best to wait until they've been sprinkled with sugar or drizzled in honey at home before you try one.

FOSSIL HUNTING

Introduction

The oldest known fossils that have ever been found were from creatures that lived 3.5 billion years ago. Hard to fathom, right? A fossil is the name given to the preserved remains of life-forms that existed on our planet in the time before recorded history. To put it simply, it is the leftover bits of something that died a very, very, VERY long time ago. There are many types of fossils to discover, although most people will immediately think of dinosaur bones. You can recognize these by their honeycomb-like structure, which is the appearance left by minerals filling in the bone marrow over time. There aren't just dinosaur bones out there, however. Fossil finds also include the human skeletons of our ancient ancestors and the tusks of Ice Age woolly mammoths, plus shells and plants and suchlike.

Why Try It?

Have you ever wondered what it would be like to share your favourite hobby with a Roman emperor? If you take up fossil hunting, you'll soon find out! The emperor Augustus loved to keep his fossil collection on full display for his guests to admire when they visited. At that time, the Romans thought that fossils were relics of mythical creatures, untamed beasts and sea monsters. To some extent, they were right. Nowadays, if you were to find a fossil that you believed had important scientific value, it would be your responsibility to report it to your local museum. That way the discovery can be appropriately studied and identified, as well as shared with the public, for anyone to visit.

Sensory Expectations

Due to the fact that one of the most common locations to find fossils is on the coast, you can expect very similar sensory inputs to other active pursuits in this book such as beachcombing. You'll definitely be getting up close and personal with lots of sedimentary rocks, so be prepared for textural encounters with grainy and gritty surfaces. Looking for patterns like the honeycomb structure of dinosaur bones or the spiral shells of ammonites can be great visual stimulation, and the soothing sound of ocean waves can have a calming aural effect.

Getting Started!

So now that you've decided to take up fossil hunting, you're going to need to choose a beach to start your search at. It would be sensible to time your visit for when the tide is falling, and also try to go in the seasons of winter or spring. But Allie, I hear you cry, won't the coast be colder during those seasons? Whilst that is a very good point, as it might well be, it's in winter or spring when the likelihood of finding a fossil is at its highest. The wind, rain and rough seas will have had the chance to scour the surface of the rocks that you'll be searching, potentially revealing hidden bones beneath. You'll definitely want to wear sturdy footwear with a grippy sole, because clambering over rocks can be dangerous. If you'd feel more confident as part of a small group, locations that are well-known for discovering fossils (such as the Jurassic Coast in England) have tour operators who can take you to the most likely spots for unearthing your own ancient find.

Support Recommendations

There are lots of hazards at the beach that you need to be aware of, so I would definitely recommend going fossil hunting with a responsible friend or family member. You need to look out for slippery rocks, crumbling cliffs, unstable ground and the rising tide. Make sure that you take enough comfortable and warm clothing if you do go in the winter time, with spares in case you accidentally plunge feet-first into a rock pool. Nobody wants to endure a miserable journey home in soggy socks!

WHERE IN THE WORLD?

As you may already know, the entire human population was once upon a time living on the continent of Africa. I'm talking tens of thousands of years ago here! Rewind to 22,000 years ago, and the Khoisan tribe of African hunter-gatherers was the largest group of humans on earth. It is thought that they may well have been the first ever people to find fossils in southern Africa, due to ancient cave paintings uncovered in that region that depict reconstructions of dinosaurs. The theory is that the Khoisan tribe imagined what these prehistoric creatures might have looked like from their discoveries of fossilized footprints and skeletal remains. Whilst the European-led archaeological expeditions to Africa in the 19th and 20th centuries are well documented, few people are aware of the first fossil hunters who roamed the continent millennia before.

GEOCACHING

Introduction

How would you feel if I told you that you could join a worldwide treasure hunt, with over 2 million secret boxes waiting to be discovered across the globe? Excited? Good, because that is exactly

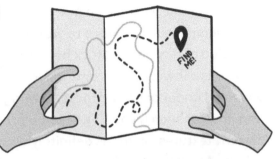

what this section is all about. Geocaching was first founded in the USA in the year 2000, and has grown to become an international phenomenon since then. Using a set of GPS coordinates (from geocaching.com or the free Geocaching smartphone app), you'll be able to find a hidden stash of treasure that most people are walking past every day without even realizing. These are known as 'caches' – waterproof boxes concealed somewhere outdoors filled with little objects and keepsakes that the geocachers before you left behind.

Why Try It?

It's worth giving geocaching a chance to be your potential new hobby because there is a lot of variety involved. A traditional cache is one that contains at least a logbook and often small treasures, whilst a multi-cache has (you guessed it!) multiple stages involved that are clues to help you reach the final location of the box. A mystery cache is even more exciting, involving puzzles that need to be solved to reveal the clues. You'll never get bored with all of those different options to explore! What is more, on geocaching.com it even notes that caches can be hidden – with permission – on both other planets and in spacecraft. So, if you get started now, you'll be an expert geocacher by the time that recreational space travel becomes the norm, and well ahead of your competition.

Sensory Expectations

As a general rule, caches are not allowed to be buried underground, which means there's no need to worry about the indescribable frustration of having soil stuck beneath your fingernails for days afterwards. However, it is common for the treasure stash to be concealed under or behind rocks, in hedges or trees, that sort of thing. In your search you'll need to be prepared to touch lots of different textures, so this is definitely a great activity for sensory seekers. An alternative for those who find walking over uneven surfaces (such as rocky ground or exposed tree roots) challenging is the 'cache and dash' approach. This is when someone drives up to a box location rather than walks there, with local lists of these types of caches available on the geocaching website and smartphone app.

Getting Started!

It is probably clear by now that you will need a smartphone or GPS device in order to begin geocaching, as this will allow you to input the location coordinates of the cache and navigate towards your treasure. Top tip: start with a traditional cache that is a regular or above on the size chart, to ensure that there is more than just a logbook inside. Should you be lucky, you might even find a geocoin! These are metal or wooden medallions created by other geocachers that you could start collecting on your travels. Once you've located the box using the GPS coordinates, write a message in the logbook and leave a keepsake for someone else to find in the future. It's a one-in-one-out rule, so if you want to take something away with you from the cache, you'll need to have brought an object of your own to replace it with.

Support Recommendations

Planning ahead is the way to overcome any anxiety and/or challenges with geocaching. First and foremost, when choosing a cache to search for, check that it is not on any DNF (Did Not Find) lists on the website or app. If it is, and multiple people have reported not having located the box, it would be best to pick a different cache. I don't know about you, but if I'd got myself excited by the prospect of treasure only to find said treasure was missing when I arrived, I'd find it pretty hard to control my emotions. Should you be geocaching with friends or family, the best approach is to decide who will be responsible for which tasks before you set off. Too many people trying to read the map at once only leads to confusion and chaos! Finally, I'd recommend having an idea of what you'd like to write in the logbook before you find it. That way you can avoid feeling pressured to come up with something fabulous on the spot.

WHERE IN THE WORLD?

If you're up for the challenge, then might I recommend putting Antarctica on your geocaching bucket list? It's the fifth largest continent on our planet and home to 49 active geocaches at the time of writing. To reach them, you'd need to face an active lava lake, a frozen grand canyon and mountains that soar to almost 5000 metres. Whilst there are no Native Antarcticans or permanent citizens of this icy landmass, visitor numbers are rising year on year. When the first geocache was placed there in 2002, average annual visitor numbers were around 15,000. Now that's increased to over 74,000! So you might want to get that trip planned quick before Antarctica becomes overrun with tourists.

HIKING

1

Introduction

Going for a hike doesn't only have to mean tackling the most technical terrain or finding the highest local hill to summit. A hike can be anything from a jaunt through the park after school to a day out on a designated trail with family or friends. It is an activity that is adaptable and accessible, with the appropriate forward planning. My dad is a wheelchair user, so we often tried to plan our hikes around trails that begin and end at the same car park, with either paved or gravel paths. Once you have your hiking boots or mobility aid, a wonderful thing about this activity is that it is then completely free. Immerse yourself in the natural world for a few hours and forget all about the stresses of homework or exams.

Why Try It?

In addition to being a great way to de-stress, hiking also offers a low impact route to improving your health and fitness. You will be getting a workout without the strain on your joints that can come with other activities like running. Plus, whilst you are out on a hike you'll be learning new skills such as navigation with a map, understanding different types of terrain and reading the weather to predict what will happen next. If you want to add a whole new level of adventure to your outings, why not also track your distances against the journeys of your favourite fictional characters? You could accompany Paddington Bear on his 6314-mile trek from Darkest Peru to London or join Bilbo Baggins on his 967-mile quest from The Shire to the Lonely Mountain.

Sensory Expectations

If you are a sensory seeker, hiking is going to be a great activity for you, because each one of your senses will be engaged along the route. However, if your senses are easily overwhelmed, you'd be best to prepare some quick solutions to common problems before setting out on your hike. If it is a sunny day, you might find that it's too

Waterproof jacket: polyester and/ or Gore-Tex

Socks: cotton, wool or bamboo, with a padded heel and toe

Hiking boots: leather or PVC leather upper with laces, padded mesh lining and rubber sole

Hiking poles: aluminium or carbon shaft with foam or rubber handgrip

bright to be comfortable, so taking a hat or sunglasses would be a wise decision. Not only would a wide-brimmed hat shelter your eyes, it would also protect the tops of your ears and back of your neck from getting burned – not at all a pleasant experience! If your local trails are anything like the ones near to where I live, there'll also be a multitude of different distracting smells all at once. Some of these can be particularly powerful, such as wild garlic here in England. If it would help, bring a handkerchief or an old T-shirt that you have spritzed with a favourite scent to hold to your nose as you walk past any smell along the route that is overpowering. Finally, another personal top tip from me: always have a raincoat or blanket that you can lay on the ground when you want to sit down if there are certain surfaces that you don't enjoy touching. I love being in green spaces, but I can't stand the sensation of grass on my skin! That way, you can sit and rest, eat a picnic or enjoy the view without feeling irritated or uncomfortable.

Getting Started!

You have probably heard before the well-known saying, 'Fail to prepare and prepare to fail'. Well, that's exactly the mindset to have when thinking about getting ready for your first hike. Success starts with packing a bag for your outing that includes the following items: a raincoat, sun hat, sunglasses, an extra layer for warmth, snacks, water, a first aid kit, portable phone charger (if relevant), torch and a map in a waterproof case. You could search online for a step-by-step route to follow in an area that you are already familiar with, using a map alongside to practise your navigational skills without having to be too concerned with getting lost. Don't worry if you don't have any proper hiking boots to start with. Instead, wear shoes that you are already comfortable walking longer distances in. Never head out on a trail in new shoes that haven't been broken in yet, because that is a sure recipe for painful blisters. If you are not going out with family or friends, make sure to tell someone where you are going and when you expect to be back, for your safety.

Support Recommendations

Having said this, it might be a good idea to go on your first hike with a more experienced friend or family member if you can. They could then share their tips and guide you along the route. If you know that there are likely to be certain challenges out on the trail that you don't feel confident facing, consider adding step-by-step instructions on how to overcome them to the notes section of your phone or in a notebook that you take with you. That way you can refer to them whenever needed. Personally, I also like to take walking poles with me on every hike, regardless of elevation. This is because walking with poles helps you to keep your balance, avoiding trips or falls that could then lead to injury.

PROFILE

Name: Holly Worton
Country: England
Activity: Hiking

How did you first get started with hiking?

I first started hiking when I was a teenager. I grew up in California and lived near the edge of the Mount Diablo State Park, and I used to go hiking in the summers and on the weekends with friends. They were happy to come along with me, but I was the one who felt compelled to get out on the trails and explore new places on the mountain.

What are the benefits that you have found from hiking?

I find that getting outdoors helps me to relax and de-stress. I spend a lot of time hiking solo, which helps me to connect with myself and get in touch with how I'm feeling and where I am in life. It brings me back to my centre.

What are the main sensory issues, if any, that you face whilst hiking?

I'm sensitive to heat, so I do most of my hiking in the spring and autumn, and I'm not as active in the outdoors during summer or winter. British weather has a bad reputation, but for me, it's perfect: not too hot or cold, and not too sunny. Just right!

My head is also sensitive to the sun; if I stay out in the sunshine for too long, I get a headache. I always bring a sun hat or scarf to keep my head cool on sunny days.

I'm also sensitive to noise, so I try to stick to quiet trails away from roads when I'm hiking and trail running. If I know that some of my route will go along a road, I make sure to bring headphones (which, for safety reasons, I only use when there's a pavement to walk on; I won't use them when walking or running in the road itself).

Spatial awareness can be an issue for me. It's improved since I started kickboxing a few years ago, but I'm not a particularly graceful person, and sometimes I trip on tree roots and stones. Hiking poles can help with this, making it much easier to stay on my feet if I trip on something.

Insect bites are very irritating to me. Thankfully, southeast England, where I live, doesn't have many biting insects. (I used to live in southeast Mexico, which had mosquitos in the wet season and biting horseflies in the dry season.) However, if I know I'll be in a place where there are mosquitos or midges, I always bring insect repellent. I'm also terrified of tick bites and Lyme disease, so I will always use insect repellent if I'm in an area that's known to have ticks, like heather or bracken.

How has being autistic impacted you (positively and/or negatively) in this activity?
In the past, I held myself back because of my fears. I didn't get diagnosed until I was 42 years old, so I spent most of my life knowing there was something different about me, but not having

the words to describe it. Once I got my diagnosis, it was easier: I better understood how my brain worked, and I was able to meet my special needs when preparing for my hiking adventures.

Since my diagnosis, I've had bigger adventures than ever before: I've hiked the South Downs Way, the Ridgeway, the Downs Link and the Wey-South Path on my own, and I'm getting ready to hike and wild camp along the Coast to Coast this year with friends. When I was training for a 100km race in 2021, I did a few training hikes where I covered more than 50km in one day with a small pack, moving quickly, as if I were racing.

Most importantly, my need to know what to expect has led me to be a safer hiker. I do loads of research before I set off on a new adventure, I prepare down to the detail, and I've taken lots of outdoor courses on navigation and other types of outdoor safety.

What advice would you give to an autistic young person who is interested in starting hiking?
Just give it a try. Get started with someone who is more experienced than you: go on an outdoors adventure course, join a Meetup group, or go with friends and family who are outdoorsy. On each adventure, pay attention to what you liked and disliked, so you can make changes and adjustments the next time you go outdoors.

Pay attention to your fears, so you can adjust your future adventures. A small step outside of your comfort zone is great because it stretches your comfort zone in the future. A huge leap outside of your comfort zone can lead to misadventure and meltdown.

Expand your adventures as your outdoor skills grow. If you feel like bigger adventures are calling you, plan to uplevel your experiences little by little. For example, I started out by hiking National Trails and staying at B&Bs, because it felt safe to walk well-marked trails and stay in a place where I could eat and shower after my walk. When I decided to upgrade my adventures to wild camping along the Coast to Coast trail – which is largely unmarked, especially in the Lake District – I arranged to hike the trail with three friends.

You might want to put together a special sensory kit for the outdoors and include things like walking poles to help with spatial recognition, a sit mat if you don't like touching the soil and tactile toys if you need to fidget with something as you hike.

Most importantly, if you feel called to start hiking, do it. But do it your way, with the accommodations you need. And grow your hiking adventures little by little.

HORSE RIDING

Introduction

Wild horses were first tamed to serve humans over 5000 years ago, probably around the region of Kazakhstan, where good horsemanship is still highly prized to this day. Over the centuries since, horses have played a vital role in human activities, from hunting to war, in addition to pulling wheeled vehicles such as wagons, carts and even chariots. Before the first steam-powered trains came along in the 19th century, if you wanted to travel across land faster than your feet could carry you, your only option was to travel by horse. Nowadays, knowing how to ride opens up far more possibilities than just a faster mode of transportation, including the chance to participate in equestrian sports like eventing, show jumping and dressage.

Why Try It?

One of my all-time favourite things that I have learned from working on this book is that horses have similar preferences to autistic folk – they like to sleep in the same stall, stick to the same habits and follow the same route whilst out and about. I've learned that they are also very happy to be guided by non-verbal communication from their rider. All in all, it sounds like the humble horse might just be an autistic person's best friend (but don't tell my dog that I said that!). Research has proven that time spent looking after and riding horses specifically supports us with reducing our negative responses to external triggers and managing excess energy. If that's not enough to convince you, then what about the chance to get involved with the Pony Club? It's an international organization with branches in 27 different countries, hosting activities such as group training sessions, camps and rallies.

Sensory Expectations

Many of the items that you will need to wear to go horse riding safely will be close-fitting: a riding hat, small-heeled boots, your clothes. The former two items might be things that you can borrow from the riding centre where your lessons are held to begin with, but bear in mind that it could take a few tries to find the kit that feels most comfortable for you and isn't applying too much pressure on your body. Another key factor to consider is the motion of riding a horse, as you will be bouncing up and down rhythmically in the saddle with the horse's movements. This motion is known to exert a calming influence on your sense of balance. It's worth highlighting that riding centres will strongly smell of a combination of leather, horse dung and hay, an aroma that definitely takes some time to get used to!

Riding boots: leather or PVC leather with rubber sole

Riding gloves: leather or PVC leather with elasticated cuffs

Riding hat: plastic or fibreglass outer shell with foam padding and nylon or PVC leather straps

Getting Started!

First, you'll want to search online to find your local riding centres or contact the Pony Club to ask for their recommendations in your area. When calling to book your first lesson, you'll be asked a few questions to allow the session to be tailored to your needs. These will likely be along the lines of whether you have any previous horse riding experience, as well as your age, height and weight (in order to match you with the most suitable horse or pony). On the day of your first lesson, it's important not to wander around the stables or through the fields but instead head straight to the reception/office area. If you aren't sure where that is, you'd be best to ask somebody on the yard for directions. During that first lesson, you'll start by meeting the horse that you will be riding before being taught by your instructor how to mount (get on) the horse. Then you will probably be led through a series of exercises to learn how to hold the reins, where to place your feet in the stirrups (which hang from the horse's saddle) and how to hold your body whilst riding. At the end of the lesson, make sure to wait until the instructor shows you how to dismount (get off) the horse safely.

Support Recommendations

For those with a disability or a long-term health condition, horse riding has historically been and continues to be a very accessible activity. Most countries will have an association or charitable organization that offers specialist sessions to accommodate additional support needs, such as the Riding for the Disabled Association in the UK. It is likely that a private or semi-private (with two to three riders in total) lesson will be the best environment to start learning in, with an additional adult to the instructor who can lead your horse and allow you to focus on practising the different commands. I would recommend asking to visit the riding centre in advance of your first lesson if that is something that you would find useful, in order to start getting used to the smells and the busyness of the yard. This way you could also meet your horse in advance, which may help calm any nerves on the day of your lesson.

PROFILE

Name: Amelia Ridley
Country: New Zealand
Activity: Horse riding

How did you first get started with horse riding?
I dreamt of having a horse when I was younger, and one day, when I was seven years old and beginning my transition into home education, I joined a home school horse riding group. I started riding with the group and it was fun. It was the happiest 3 hours of my week and it was something I really looked forward to. It was the first activity I found that I enjoyed and wanted to go back to week after week. My parents and I quickly realized this was not only something I thoroughly enjoyed, but I was actually quite good at it. Horse riding felt comfortable to me. Suddenly my 'unhorsey' parents and I were immersed into a world that we all knew nothing about. The three of us learned very quickly, however, when we were gifted a retired rescue pony named Maddy, who was in desperate need of some love...

What are the benefits that you have found from horse riding?
I find it easier to socialize with people now as I can talk about something I'm interested in. I have made friends with other kids and adults who like horses. Now I can do a sport and be part of a Pony Club. I also find it easier to fall asleep at night because I

can think about my horses. I have seven now. George, Opal, Zara, Pete, Spice, Athena and Dot. I absolutely love my horses and I find them calming (mostly).

Dressage is my favourite event. With dressage you can learn and practise the test in your own environment. Then, at the competition, you have an exact time allocated so you know exactly what to do and when you will be doing it. This helps to reduce some anxiety because I can prepare myself for what is to come. This is unlike a show jumping competition where you have no idea what the jumps or the arena will look like until the day.

What are the main sensory issues, if any, that you face whilst horse riding?
There are many sensory issues in horse riding; however, there are certainly ways to manage these and it's well worth doing as the riding is so rewarding. These are some of the sensory struggles I personally have, but I've also found good solutions to them.

It's difficult for me to find equestrian clothes that are comfortable. At equestrian competitions and Pony Club you need to wear certain clothes. I can't wear jodhpurs like other kids as I hate the feel of them, so I can only wear certain brands of riding tights, and often we have a lot of trouble finding the right ones. Comfortable riding socks are also hard to find as they all have sparkles in them, which are itchy and very annoying, plus riding boots are hard and bulky. Also, the seam from the toes on the boot digs into my feet, which is extra annoying. Once we find socks and boots I can wear comfortably we buy a few pairs. I also can't stand the feeling of the reins when I'm riding or the lead rope, so I must wear gloves, and I'm so pleased I have found comfortable ones now. Although these clothing items are a real sensory issue for me, once I find the right gear I really love my riding outfits and it feels nice to wear them.

There are always lots of people, horses, noise and announcements at equestrian events and it can be a lot to process for me. I find noises and bright colours distracting. Once there was a small bright flapping flag on the side of the competition arena and I couldn't concentrate, which made me angry. When these things are irritating me I will chew the inside of my mouth, which then hurts for the next week. These are things I have become aware of and I love riding my horse and competing so much that I do try my best to block these things out so I can enjoy my outing. This takes practice but is well worth it. With my dressage it is okay because I can focus on what I have learned and I know exactly what I am there to do.

How has being autistic impacted you (positively and/or negatively) in this activity?
I found this question a bit hard to answer as I can't separate being autistic from myself. I have very high expectations and my perfectionism causes anxiety and can then impact negatively on my practice. I like to do things right the first time and I don't leave myself any room for mistakes, so I can get very upset when I'm trying to perfect a test and it isn't going the way I imagined it would.

I do think noises impact me more than other people, and this can affect my horse riding negatively as they distract me and I can't concentrate. When I go to a competition I can't warm my pony up in the warm-up arena as there are other ponies in there and I feel like they might run into me or get too close to me. I can't judge where the other ponies are going to move to and I get overwhelmed, causing my anxiety to flare up so that I can't concentrate, and that's when I get very angry. To try and help this I warm my pony up at home if we are going to a local show or I find a quiet corner to warm up in if I can (this isn't always possible so my warm up might not be very good, but at least then I have managed to stay calmer before my event starts).

With so much out of my control I get scared and start to think something bad will happen or that I can't ride, which makes me lose my confidence. Horses can sense how I feel and my anxiety, and if I don't feel too confident, then they feel less confident also. I struggle with my confidence and this is probably due to anxiety. I'm not sure what anxiety levels other riders have, but mine are quite high. My brain doesn't stop thinking about all the things that can go wrong when I'm riding. I do know I have more struggles than other kids that ride, and often people have asked me if I actually enjoy riding as I have trouble showing positive emotions. My answer to that is that autistic people are more difficult to read apparently and, yes, we absolutely have more struggles, but I love my horse riding and the positives outweigh all the negatives that come with it.

I don't like travelling to new places and often going to competitions causes me to have to function at peak anxiety, when something really small can be enough to scare me or make me worried to compete. On the days following a competition or an outing I need to stay home and not go out of the house other than to see my horses, just to try and return to feeling okay.

From a positive perspective I now know I have an amazing connection with horses. They are what I've found makes me happy. I take pride in things that I have achieved like winning ribbons and learning new dressage tests and skills. I just won the Pony Club dressage award for the year. I feel good that I know that I have something that I am truly good at and that I can control how far I want to go in the sport, but also that I can just have a day hacking out or at the river with the horses, and it is not always just about practising or getting better. It is about adventures and using horses as a reason to go and have them and experience more with my friends and of course my special horse friends.

What advice would you give to an autistic young person who is interested in starting horse riding?
Try it, and if it's something you enjoy, keep going. Some days are very hard with horses, but if you enjoy the good times, keep going. What I look forward to most at the moment is my horse adventures with my friends, so joining a horse riding group would be a good start. You don't have to compete; you can just have gentle rides or go on treks. Or you can enter showing competitions where you don't ride; you just make them look good. Or you don't even have to enter competitions; you can just make them look pretty, just for you! There is something for everyone with horses, and they have certainly made my life better.

I do hope to compete at the Olympics in dressage one day, but for now I just look forward to the endless horse adventures with my friends. What riding does for me is like nothing else in the world – it makes me feel so good.

KAYAKING

Introduction

If you want to get around using a mode of transport that's existed for at least 4000 years, then kayaking might be for you. These lightweight boats are human powered using a double-bladed paddle and differ from canoes in that they have a deck covering the hull. Traditionally, in the sub-Arctic regions of the earth where these craft originated, they were built from collected driftwood and covered in seal or other animal skins stitched together. Whilst I love going kayaking, I have to be honest and admit I don't think I could sit in one made out of seal skin...

Why Try It?

Since that time, plastic kayaks have been developed that allow for stronger and smaller models. This has led to a range of different kayaking disciplines emerging, so there really is something for everyone. I personally enjoy sea or lake kayaking (staying near to the shore, mind you!), but you could also try freestyle, surf, racing or whitewater kayaking, if any of those take your fancy. Should you decide that this is the sport for you, it's possible to support your performance on the water by including other activities like running and swimming into your training routine. Getting interested in kayaking could be the gateway to an overall fitter lifestyle!

Sensory Expectations

Take a quick peek at the sensory expectations for canoeing, as these will be very similar. For kayaking specifically, it's worth highlighting that you may well have a spray deck attached to your boat, which is a neoprene waterproof cover that sits around your waist. This acts as a barrier to stop water hitting your lower body or filling up the inside of the kayak. The sensation of using one will definitely take some getting used to! To minimize the sensory input that you receive from the water, make sure to choose somewhere calm at first, like a bay on the coast or a slow-moving river.

Buoyancy aid: nylon outer shell, PVC padding, elasticated sides and nylon straps

Helmet: plastic shell, foam padding and nylon strap

Paddle: aluminium shaft

Getting Started!

If you have friends or family who are experienced kayakers, you could learn by going out on the water with them and borrowing or hiring the appropriate kit. If that is not an option for you, there is likely to be a local club or activity centre offering taster sessions and/or lessons that you can take part in. Before you set off, check the weather together to ensure that it is safe to kayak, as the wind speed can make it really dangerous to be out on the water. Pack water and safe food snacks to keep you energized and hydrated on world. I began by attending club sessions on Saturday mornings that soon progressed to Tuesday and Thursday evenings as well by the end of that summer. The following April I did my first proper sprint race at the National Water Sports Centre in Nottingham. I raced in Boys D, which was the lowest racing division as it was my first regatta, but by the end of that racing season I had progressed to Boys A, the highest racing division. I still to this day hold the record for the fastest progression in British kayaking history through the racing ranks.

That year solidified what kayaking meant to me and what it did for my life in general, so I made the decision to carry on paddling and see where it would take me. Having struggled at school and with my home life after being diagnosed with dyslexia, dyspraxia, sensory integration disorder and dyscalculia, it was a total release when I went paddling and got myself away from academic life. When I first started kayaking, I was medically considered morbidly obese, but I lost a lot of weight within that year. My body confidence had grown massively, with a total change in my physique and mentality.

What are the benefits that you have found from kayaking?
Kayaking gave me a sense of direction and purpose, as it got me away from school and the worries and hardships that came from struggling in education. Kayaking also gave me a massive sense of confidence. Because I had really struggled with school and constantly felt hard done by, it was the first time in my life that I was achieving something I was working towards. The fitness gave me the body confidence that I had lacked in my younger years after I had stopped swimming. Kayaking also gave me a community who accepted me for who I was, with people who wanted to help me and see me achieve. I had gone from the bullied child at school to the feared racer when I got on the start line. I underestimated the power of sport and what

your adventure, plus a whistle so that in an emergency others can easily hear where you are.

Support Recommendations

If you need to, take extra time to practise safety drills in shallow waters before heading out properly in your kayak. It's important that you feel confident handling the boat and responding to any unexpected situations, so never feel pressured to move on before you are ready. Sometimes it can take longer for our autistic brains to fully understand and remember something, and that's okay! To start with, I'd suggest making sure the instructor or your more experienced friend or family member has a towline with them when you go out on the water. That way, if you begin to feel overwhelmed or even just tired, they can tow you back to shore in their kayak.

PROFILE
Name: Chris Carson
Country: England
Activity: Kayaking

How did you first get started with kayaking?
I started kayaking when I was 15 years old, which was a natural

Photo credit: Ian Wrighton Photography

progression as I had spent most of my childhood in a swimming pool whilst my mother coached swim squads. I sadly fell out of love with any kind of sport, finding myself in a place of not doing any exercise around the age of 13–14 years old. I had loved water sports and had loved being outside but had no way of doing it, so when I found kayaking, it was like a door was unlocked to a new it could do for someone, not just in their sporting life but their whole lifestyle and outlook. I had finally found my purpose that wasn't defined by any disability. I was asked continually how my disabilities would affect my paddling, especially my dyspraxia; however, I actually found that the kayaking helped me and was never inhibited by these disabilities to almost any extent. I couldn't catch a ball or track any moving object for the life of me when I was at school, but when I found kayaking, it was again like I had unlocked the secret to my disability. I actually feel as though the extra sensitivities that I have helped me adapt and learn the technique required to kayak, and I believe this to be why I progressed so quickly in the sport.

In addition, the confidence and lifestyle/structure that I had gained from the full-time training allowed me to believe in myself enough that I then pursued education to university level. I had left school with six GCSEs and two A Levels, all around the borderline of failing. This was a massive blow to my confidence; however, kayaking during a gap year after school and doing well in this gap year gave me the confidence to tackle education for one last time. I went back to college to get the equivalent of two more A-Levels/a foundation degree to allow me access to university. I managed this by having the structure of training and the discipline to sit and study, using paddling as a release. Four years later I have a first-class undergraduate degree in Psychology and am currently completing my Master's degree in Social Psychology at the University of Surrey.

What are the main sensory issues, if any, that you face whilst kayaking?

Kayaking does require a mindset, and it is one that I have had to teach myself and work on every day. My inability to count and work with numbers has affected my timekeeping during sessions and my memory of what the session is (e.g., how many sets and intervals the coach sets out for us to do). So, I write these on the deck of my boat with a whiteboard marker before every session. My sensitivities from my sensory integration disorder affect me during the winter whilst being wrapped up at 0°C. I would struggle with different fabrics during my childhood, and when I started kayaking, the feeling of heavy clothing when wet was totally overwhelming. My short-term memory problems would be a nightmare when remembering the racecourse or how many laps we had to do during a race or even just training sessions. I couldn't be given more than a maximum of two instructions during a technique session, or I would forget them and become distracted. My dyslexia hadn't affected me that much during my kayaking until I started to attend international events where foreign languages would come into play. The admin of getting onto the trip and the reading of pages of official documents or race rules would flummox me.

As I mentioned before, I actually found the kayaking to have a calming effect on my dyspraxia; however, I do still shake, and this is exacerbated during heavy gym sessions. Despite all of this, I don't even consider any of these as issues anymore, because kayaking has taught me to cope with them, live with them and enjoy them as unique components of myself. I find they have made me who I am. I sit on the start line of a race and feel as though I had to work a little bit harder than the rest of my competitors to get there. And that is a great feeling to have.

How has being autistic impacted you (positively and/or negatively) in this activity?
Being a spectrum, autism has affected me in many different ways. However, retrospectively, I now see it as a blessing in disguise. I have worked hard to deal with these issues and now find it to be a sense of achievement. It still didn't make it easy to live with and deal with at the time, though.

What advice would you give to an autistic young person who is interested in starting kayaking?

My three takeaways from my experiences with sport are:

- Put yourself out there. You'll never find your limits of what you are capable of until you try. It won't be easy and you will fail. But it will be worth it in the end.
- Give yourself structure and purpose. Find what you love and make it an obsession. Your autism will definitely help with this. Live, breathe and be totally engrossed in that activity. Learn everything about it, and spend the time working on it more than anyone else.
- Be kind to yourself, because it will be hard and you will have to work harder than anyone else. Yet your autism thrives off structure, so give yourself the structure and give yourself the routine of doing sport. It will be worth it.

LARPING

Introduction

Back in 1977, a guy called Bryan advertised on American radio that he was looking for people to join him 'to fight in Hobbit wars with padded weapons'. Most people agree that this was the start of LARPing (Live Action Role Playing), where someone plays a specific character in an imaginary world and reacts to the plot or the actions of others around them in real time. It has even been suggested that this activity dates back as far as the 16th century, when the court of Henry VIII re-enacted the adventures of Robin Hood for fun. Nowadays LARPing communities can be found across the world, each one collaboratively creating its own characters, backstory and settings.

Why Try It?

LARPing is one of the most interesting entries in this book, in the sense that it's so easy to see the ways that getting involved could directly benefit your life as an autistic person. Being part of a LARPing community gives you the chance to make friends with others who share common interests, whilst also helping you to learn social skills and how to express yourself. As a beginner player, you improvise your character's decisions and actions by observing what others around you are doing and matching their responses. This is exactly how most autistic people manage social interactions in their everyday lives! So LARPing provides a safe space to practise that skill, make mistakes and learn from them.

Sensory Expectations

There are a number of ways that you can tailor this activity to suit your sensory preferences. First, there's your costume. Many LARPers will make their own, which means that you can choose whatever fabrics and styles you find most comfortable to wear. Second, there's the environment. Regardless of if you choose to role-play alone, with friends or family, or with an organized group, you can decide where to go and thereby avoid any sensory inputs that you find irritating or distracting. Third, there's the group size. As you would expect, the bigger the group, the more noise and visual stimulation involved in the LARP. If having a lot going on around you all at once is going to be too overwhelming, that's when having a go alone or with a small selection of friends or family might be the better option.

Getting Started!

You can start LARPing today: in your back garden, local park, forest... All you need is your imagination to dream up a character and a situation to put them in. Many of us already played like this when we were younger! Otherwise, you can look for a nearby community to join, by searching online for a website or social media page. Popular places to hold games include local parks, forests, camping grounds and sports fields.

Support Recommendations

The main skill you'll use and develop is improvisation. It will be a rewarding challenge to face, so give yourself the best chance of success. If you choose to join a community rather than LARP alone, consider speaking to the director about having extra guidance and support in the beginning. Maybe your character could have a mentor, a more experienced player who helps them make decisions and take actions until you feel more confident. Or you could LARP alone and channel your inner Merida (from Pixar's film *Brave*), as I have always wanted to do!

WHERE IN THE WORLD?

If you are a Harry Potter fan, then you need look no further than the 13th-century Czocha Castle in Poland for the LARP of your dreams. There lies the College of Wizardry, an annual (unofficial!) recreation of life at Hogwarts. Over the space of a weekend, you take on an assigned student character and attend a timetable of lessons based on your chosen path: guardian, healer, curse breaker, artificer or cryptozoologist. There are even clubs and secret societies, with intriguing names like the 'Ancient Order of Mischief' and 'Explorers of the Eternal'. For anyone who has ever finished a Harry Potter film or book and sighed with disappointment that they, too, weren't spending their days casting spells and drinking butterbeer, fear not – your prayers have been answered.

LOCAL EXPLORATION

Introduction

Here's a wild thought for you – have you ever considered planning a day out in your own hometown or neighbouring city? It's really easy to fall into thinking that we know everything there is to know about where we live, simply because we live there. Yet how many of you could tell me how your hometown was founded, or why? Have you visited the local tourist hotspots yourself or just seen them on someone else's social media? Taking the time to explore where

you live on foot (or human-powered transport) is not only a sure-fire way to learn more about your local area, but it will also get you active and give your immune system a boost. What's not to like about that?

Why Try It?

You've probably heard of FOMO: it's an acronym for Fear Of Missing Out. It's funny to think that you've likely never experienced FOMO in the context of spending a day out in your hometown or city, because I can guarantee that there'll definitely be things that you've missed out on! I do, however, have some tips on what you can do to make sure that you're not missing out anymore. Try walking along a route that you would usually drive or be driven on, to notice the small details that get overlooked when you are staring out of a car window. You could even invite a friend or family member from a different part of the country (or even the world) to come and visit, allowing you to see your local area from a new perspective as you show them around. If you're not that bothered about missing out, how about expanding your local knowledge? Learning more about where you live allows you to develop deeper ties with your home and connect to the wider community that has lived there throughout the ages.

Sensory Expectations

Now here's where things begin to get really interesting. Throughout this book, I've been making recommendations about how to mitigate certain sensory experiences that you might encounter whilst participating in a particular activity. For this section, that's going to be your job instead! I obviously have no idea what kind of place you live in, so this is a chance for you to write your own guide that other people can use to learn about the sensory expectations of your local area. What sights are there? What smells are there? What sounds are there? What tastes are there? What textures are there?

Getting Started!

There are so many different ways that you could start exploring your hometown or city that I thought I'd create a little checklist for you to tick things off as you try them:

- ☐ Go on a hop-on, hop-off bus tour (you know, the ones that the tourists use!).
- ☐ Look in a local newspaper for special events or activities that might be on.
- ☐ Search for bloggers online who have visited your local area, and try one of their recommendations.

- Join a free walking tour to learn more about the historical background of your home town or city.
- No walking tour? No problem! Have a look out for information panels by parks, high streets, historic sites and marketplaces to create a self-guided route.
- Embark on a selfie treasure hunt and aim to visit all of the locations nearby that always feature in tourists' holiday photographs.
- If you need more inspiration, perhaps there is a film or book that was set where you live – you could watch or read it, and then go find some of the places that are mentioned.

If you are heading out with friends, make sure that a parent or guardian has a copy of your itinerary so they know where you're going to be throughout the day.

Support Recommendations

If you are someone who feels a bit daunted by the prospect of heading out for the day and seeing what happens (that's me!), then I have some advice for you. So as not to become overwhelmed by decision fatigue during your local adventuring, why not create an itinerary just as you would for visiting somewhere further away? You and your family or friends can schedule in ticketed activities such as the bus, historic sites and museum tours, as well as flexible activities like the selfie treasure hunt or self-guided walking tour. It's important that you also remember to include downtime between the different activities – either simply to rest or to ensure that you stay fed and hydrated!

ALLIE'S FIRST ATTEMPT

During the summer holidays my brother and his friends would

go on long bike rides together in the local countryside, leaving after breakfast and not getting back until dinner was being served in the evening. I distinctly remember that there was one time I decided to do something similar, but on my own. There was a road out of our little market town that we called Back Lane, which usually formed part of a short cycling loop that we did sometimes. I had never followed the road all the way to the end to see where it led, however. So that day, I packed up a picnic and set out to discover what lay at the end of Back Lane. This was before I ever had a smartphone with Google Maps (which now I can't imagine not having access to!). It turns out that after a mere 2 miles I reached a very small village with more trees than houses. Not the biggest of adventures, but I'd still discovered somewhere new.

MUDLARKING

Introduction

Once upon a time in Victorian England, searching for treasures in the mud was a formally recognized profession called 'mudlarking'. It was mostly carried out by children, especially boys, who spent their days looking along the riverbanks for items that could be sold on for profit, providing a stream (see what I did there?!) of income for their families. Wherever a river was used as a trade route or for recreational travel, there you would find 'mudlarks' earning a living. The objects that they looked for were possessions that people had been losing or discarding in rivers for thousands of years. In Victorian England, mudlarking was a very dangerous profession to be in, however, with a high risk of injury or catching waterborne diseases due to the conditions at the time. In the 21st century, however, it has become a popular hobby in much the same way as beachcombing.

Why Try It?

A great way to think about mudlarking in our modern age is as accessible archaeology. You don't need a fancy qualification or expensive equipment to be able to find a little piece of history; you can simply visit your local river and have a go for yourself (just check you don't need a permit first!). The mud along the foreshore acts as an anaerobic preservative. This means that, when you pick up an interesting object – perhaps from as far back as the Mesolithic period (around 8000 BCE!) – it will still look very similar to how it was on the day that it was first lost to the river. Mudlarking gives you the chance to hold in your very own hands the possessions of ordinary people like us, who lived hundreds or even thousands of years ago.

Sensory Expectations

A key component in the mudlarking experience is going to be your vision. In order to discover these historic objects, you'll want to be looking out for predictable patterns, straight lines and perfect circles, as those are indicative of a man-made artefact. There will be other sensory inputs, too, in the forms of the sounds and smells of the river, as well as the sticky and squelchy mud itself. Most mudlarkers nowadays wear disposable gloves to protect themselves against catching waterborne diseases, so you may also have to deal with the texture of rubber or vinyl against your skin.

Getting Started!

In addition to disposable gloves, there are a few other things that you'll need before you begin mudlarking. These are walking boots or wellington boots (because the ground will be wet and muddy), a bucket or similar receptacle (to collect your treasures in!) and a set of knee pads (to protect your knees from the damp, uneven ground). As I alluded to earlier when I highlighted the importance of vision, mudlarkers start with searching 'by eye'. However, if you get really invested in this activity, you could always introduce tools such as a trowel or sieve to help you unearth the more buried artefacts.

Support Recommendations

As with beachcombing, it's essential that you are prepared and safe so that you can enjoy the best possible experience. Be aware of the hazards around you. These could include the rising tide if the river is located near the sea, or slippery steps if the river is in a town or city centre. Should you be aware that you are likely to hyperfocus whilst doing this activity, I'd recommend taking a friend or family member with you to help on the lookout for any potential hazards. You're supposed to be rescuing things from the river, not needing to be rescued yourself! On that note, if you are going alone, do remember to always let a parent or guardian know where you're headed.

WHERE IN THE WORLD?

Now this is a story that will warm your heart. Back in the summer of 2020, a mudlarker came across a dirt-encrusted 19th-century halfpenny whilst using his metal detector along a towpath beside the River Thames in London. He could tell that the coin was hand engraved with some words, but it wasn't until he got home and was able to clean it that he realized those words were a name and address. After a bit of online sleuthing, he managed to trace the last known address of the grandson of the man whose name was on the coin. He sent him a letter and within a month had a reply; the halfpenny had been used as a dog tag, and with the letter was enclosed a black and white photograph from the 1930s of the man, holding his grandson, with the very dog stood at his feet! It turned out that the tag had been lost on a walk decades earlier, with nobody ever expecting that it would be found again, especially after so much time had passed.

NATURE WRITING 1

Introduction

Nature writing is all about using words to explore the aspects of the world around us that weren't made by human hands. It can take many forms, from the factual to the poetic, and can often be found in books such as field guides, memoirs and essays on natural history. Centuries ago, nature was simply considered a setting, in narratives like hunting stories, fables and traveller's tales. Today, however, nature has very much become the subject in its own right.

Why Try It?

You might think that, in order to write about nature, you need to take yourself off to wild and formidable places, to remove yourself from society completely and become one with great mountains or vast oceans. I'm here to tell you that that is definitely not necessary. Nature writing is a chance to explore your personal relationship with Mother Earth, be that in a wild place far from home or right where you live. Leaves poking up through the pavement, angry clouds in a stormy sky or the hedgehog that likes to stop by in your back garden are all examples of potential inspiration. You'll be amazed at what you notice around you when you really focus on looking.

Sensory Expectations

Whilst you're writing in the great outdoors, I would recommend having your preferred sensory supports with you so that you can self-regulate if you begin to feel overwhelmed. That could be sunglasses for bright sunshine, ear defenders for loud and/or background noises or a favourite fidget toy to provide a reassuring texture, to name only a few suggestions. Bringing something familiar with you when you are planning to try something new is always, in my opinion, a sensible idea. I'd also recommend taking a look at the sensory expectations for drawing, as there will be a lot of overlap when it comes to the different materials that you can choose to write with/on.

Getting Started!

If you have something to write with or on, whether that be analogue or digital, you have everything that you need to start nature writing. Whilst I personally use a pen or pencil and a notebook, you may prefer to type or even dictate into your smartphone, if you have one. The only other requirement to begin is to find a place that you would like to write about. Remember, nature is all of the world around you that wasn't made by human hands. Animals, plants and the elements exist in the city streets just as much as the open countryside. Find your place, take out your paper or digital device, and get writing.

Support Recommendations

Sometimes it can feel daunting to try something new without having seen how somebody else does it first. If that's how you're feeling about nature writing, then look no further than Dara McAnulty. Dara is an autistic naturalist who writes about his relationship with the wild, describing what he sees, hears, smells, tastes and touches in vivid detail. His first book, *Diary of a Young Naturalist*, could help you to feel more confident to give nature writing a try by reading parts of it first.

ALLIE'S FIRST ATTEMPT

Although I have been writing creatively since early childhood, I didn't properly give nature writing a go until very recently. Back in 2020, I bought a notebook with a rather majestic peacock on the front and a different animal illustration on every page. It really is a thing of beauty. I started to use it to record my observations when I was out walking in nature, whether that be a stroll around the local park or a long woodland hike. Sometimes these musings weren't even full sentences, but snippets of thoughts. Other times, they read almost like a conversation with myself: 'I love the way that the world smells during and after it rains. I need to find that bottled in a candle somewhere.' Since working on this book I've fallen out of the habit of using my nature writing notebook, but it's something I very much look forward to returning to.

ORIENTEERING

Introduction

It was first in the Swedish military in 1886 that the term 'orienteering' was used, to describe the act of traversing unfamiliar terrain with the help of a map and a compass. Fast-forward four decades from then and this activity began to be recognized as a recreational sport, expanding initially across Scandinavia, into Europe and the rest of the world. By 1966, it was possible to compete internationally in orienteering, at the World Championships. The sport comprises of using a bespoke map to navigate between designated checkpoints,  usually in numerical order. These bespoke maps illustrate the terrain in a high level of detail with symbols and colour coding. Most have a key or legend included to help participants to understand the meaning of the different symbols and colours.

Why Try It?

You can begin orienteering at any age, with any level of fitness. It's an activity that benefits both the body and the mind, through movement and intellectual stimulation respectively. Problem-solving is a key aspect, from identifying your current location on the map to figuring out the best route to reach the next checkpoint. In addition, orienteering encourages the development of map reading and navigational skills, which can only be a good thing in an age when we rely so much on our smartphones to get us from A to B. There are many types of course to choose from to start developing these skills, including permanent courses that use posts and plaques as checkpoints. These would be the ideal places to return to at different times during your orienteering hobby, to compare how quickly you can locate the checkpoints as your map-reading abilities improve – a fun and easy way to measure how far you have progressed!

Sensory Expectations

Speaking of getting quicker the more that you practise, it's worth noting that orienteering – especially at a competitive level – can involve a lot of running, so it's definitely worth referring to that section in this book for related sensory expectations. Don't be disheartened, however, if you are a wheelchair user, as there are trail orienteering competitions designed specifically for participants of all physical abilities to compete on equal terms. With regards to the clothing worn, this usually consists of a lightweight top and Lycra leggings to facilitate an easy range of motion, but as this is not compulsory to taking part, you can absolutely wear whatever types and materials of clothing that you feel most comfortable in. It's also worth noting that you can orienteer on a bike, horse, skis and even in a canoe, so these sections are probably useful to refer to if you decide to try one of those variations.

Getting Started!

Whether you are a city dweller or a country bumpkin, there'll be plenty of places to start orienteering near you. One option is to join a local club if you have one, as these often hold training sessions for beginners that you can get involved with. This is a good choice for those who don't own a compass, because a club will have spares that you can borrow. As a beginner, you'll be wanting to follow courses that are colour-coded white, yellow or orange, due to their shorter length and more visible checkpoints. Should there not be a club local to you, another option is to search online for permanent courses set in a nearby forest, town centre, park or university campus.

Support Recommendations

As you'll be expected to reach your own conclusions about which route to follow to find each checkpoint, orienteering might prove particularly challenging for anyone who struggles with executive dysfunction. This is when you find it harder to plan, pay attention, remember information and/or multi-task. If you'd still like to have a go regardless, the good news is that orienteering in a small team is commonplace, even at competitive levels. Much like with geocaching, a beneficial approach would be to designate different tasks – such as map reading, identifying terrain type and navigating – to different members of your team.

WHERE IN THE WORLD?

How many checkpoints do you think that you could find in 100 minutes? Okay, but what about if you were running up and down a Swiss mountain to find them? Right. And do you think you'd be able to find one of the checkpoints if it was pinned to a man in a bear costume? That's what the competitors of the Red Bull Alptitude race face, with a penalty of 15 points deducted for every minute that they are late back to the finishing line. Whilst it sounds like a gruelling challenge, I'm sure you'd enjoy the green meadows and snowy peaks of the host Swiss mountain resort of Arosa during the race. Plus, there's always the cows cheering you on along the route!

PHOTOGRAPHY

Introduction

The world's first photograph was
taken of the view from a French
scientist's window in 1826. Less than
two decades later, in 1843, the first
photographically illustrated book
was produced in Britain – about
algae! Thankfully, photography
has developed a lot since the 19th
century (pun intended), and many
other interesting subjects have
been captured on camera since.
Before colour photography was
invented, people used to hand paint

over the important features of a print, such as the eyes and lips on
portraits. This probably seems like a lot of work compared to how
easily we edit, filter and enhance our photographs today!

Why Try It?

As I researched this section I read a number of interviews with
autistic photographers and it quickly became clear that they viewed
photography as an outlet for expression. This was especially true
for the times when they couldn't find the right words, or words
themselves weren't enough, to convey how they were feeling.
Not only that, but the photographs that they then created were
considered by others to offer a unique perspective on a composition
or subject that those without autistic brains might never have

noticed. It's well worth trying photography if you would like to explore different ways of communicating beyond the traditional verbal and written options.

Sensory Expectations

The type of camera that you decide to use will have sensory implications. Taking photographs on a smartphone, for example, might feel very familiar, whereas a DSLR camera will be heavier, more cumbersome to hold and will require you to use a viewfinder. It's worth noting as well that you are likely to spend more time in lighter and brighter locations in order to take the best photographs. (Unless dark and moody is the vibe that you are going for, of course!)

Getting Started!

Once you have the equipment to begin taking photographs, you're ready to go! There are far too many different types of camera for me to be able to go into detail here, but some of the options that you might consider are: smartphone, digital camera, disposable film camera or DSLR camera. Much like choosing a subject for nature writing, the only other requirement is to decide what you would like to photograph. As you spend more time practising, you might want to learn further about the practical and/or artistic aspects of the hobby. You could potentially do this through a variety of mediums, from completing an online course to watching online videos from professionals to joining a local club in your town or at your school.

Support Recommendations

If you feel intimidated by the idea of heading out with a camera for the first time, why not seek inspiration from the work of some other autistic photographers first? You could take a look at Alfie Bowen's portraits of animals, or Joe James' landscapes. Both of these men have had their work published, so you can search for examples online. I would also recommend taking your preferred sensory supports along with your camera of choice, so that you are well prepared to self-regulate if you begin to feel overwhelmed.

PROFILE

Name: Alex Heron
Country: England
Activity: Photography

How did you first get started with photography?

I have always loved photography; one of my first memories is taking photographs of my sister when she was born. I was three years old at the time and I used my parents' big film camera! I used to get overwhelmed easily by sounds and the environment I was in, so I would carry a small film camera around with me and take pictures of random things. My parents would then take the film to be developed, and when the prints came back I would safely store and sort them in photo albums. I did this all the time growing up, and then I moved on to a digital camera when I was about nine years old. I studied photography at GCSE and A-Level and it was my favourite subject – I did really well in it. When I was 16, my grandad became very poorly and was in a special hospital; I find expressing emotion extremely difficult, but I found one of his old film cameras and took it to him and we used it together whilst he was ill. It really helped me to bond with my grandad, by doing something together that we both love.

What are the benefits that you have found from photography?

Photography has helped me in so many ways – I think doing

something you love every day is the key to life. It means you get to grow and develop with your interest, and when someone really loves a subject, they are usually really good at it, because they are so passionate about it and dedicate so much time to it. I have always thought in pictures instead of words – my thoughts are like a rolling movie 24/7, so photography is kind of like showing the world what inside my brain looks like! The biggest benefit to photography, for me, is that it has enabled me to socialize in ways I never thought I could. I find social situations very difficult. I never know what to say and I get easily overwhelmed. Photography has really helped me with this because I get to meet people every day when I am taking their photograph. The best thing about meeting people to photograph them is that they are there because they really want their photo taken, so I can talk about my special interest and passion with them, and they are genuinely interested. Therefore, I don't have to worry about what to say or making small talk – I can just talk about my love of photography!

I also find being in busy or crowded environments nearly impossible, but for some reason, if I have been asked to take photographs, I can be anywhere and cope really well. I think it is because photography allows me to go into my own world. It's like all of the noises and the crowd drifts away and it's just me and my camera.

What are the main sensory issues, if any, that you face whilst taking photographs?
Luckily, for me, photography tends to reduce any sensory issues from the environment I'm in, as I just go into a hyperfocus of my own photography world. It kind of feels like I'm flying above the room, with all the noises and lights far below me – I can barely hear it! However, I am extremely sensitive to heat and I find being in a studio with big lights very hot, so I make sure I go outside

and walk around if I feel myself getting too stressed. My camera is very big, so sometimes I find walking around big cities with my camera in its bag a bit stressful, especially if it is crowded!

How has being autistic impacted you (positively and/or negatively) in this activity?

I have thought about this question a lot throughout my career and I have never been able to come up with a definitive answer. I think it's because I've always been autistic, so I don't know what it is like to not be autistic. If I could live for a day without autism, I could probably answer this question a lot better, as I'd have something to compare to. From my own experience, I think autism has allowed me to pursue photography with an immense level of focus, drive and passion. I have been given an ability to chase my dreams wholeheartedly and a drive to work on my photography every single day without fail. I also think that, due to my autistic brain thinking in pictures, pictures and photography make sense to me, and always have done. It kind of feels like photography shows people a glimpse of how I see and think about the world, which I find hard to express in words.

I have also always found expressing emotion very difficult. As a child I was always labelled as 'cold' or distant. I don't say much and I don't like hugs, so I find it hard to show the people I love how much I love them. Photography has helped me do that, because when I take a picture of my family, I try to capture the things about them that I love so much, and then I get to keep that image forever, like my very own piece of time. I get to show people the way that I see them and the things I love about them.

What advice would you give to an autistic young person who is interested in starting photography?

My biggest piece of advice is always photograph what you love! When people photograph what they love, you can feel that through their images. Your passion will shine through; you are showing people the way that you see the world and the things that you love – that's a story that only you can tell! It's really hard when you are starting out, as maybe your equipment isn't the best, and not many people are seeing your work; there is always going to be a better, more expensive camera you can use, but it doesn't matter. A good photograph is a good photograph – it doesn't matter what camera was used to take it. Take as many photos as you possibly can, search online for tutorials and dedicate at least 10 minutes every day to learning more about photography! I think the main thing that helped me, and still helps me, to improve is to constantly look at photographs that inspire me and at the work of photographers that I aspire to be like. Constantly looking at new images from photographers that you look up to will really help shape your own work. I would really urge new photographers to have a go at shooting on a film camera. It can be expensive, so you have to be careful not to take too many photos at once, but learning to shoot on a film camera gives you a great technical ability. My last piece of advice is to never ever feel intimidated by any camera you use. They are all the same and do the same thing; they just have buttons in different places! Being autistic means you have a unique perspective of the world, and that is so inspiring.

ROLLER SKATING

Introduction

An eccentric Belgian inventor was the brains behind the roller skate, first designed in 1743 to help actors mimic ice skating on stage in the theatre. Fast-forward to 1863 and an American inventor brought the roller skate to a wider audience, marketing skating as an appropriate way for young men and women to spend time together without a chaperone. Nowadays roller skating is as much a sport as a recreational activity, with the World Skate Games having nine different disciplines that it is possible to compete in. This activity has seen a rise in popularity on social media, where teens are posting videos of themselves dancing on roller skates to music.

Why Try It?

I may be biased, considering that roller skating is my sport of choice, but nothing beats that feeling of freewheeling on your own two feet. Your skates begin to feel like an extension of your own body that allows you to move faster and glide across the surface of roads and pavements. When I'm roller skating, clichés come true in that the world around me fades as I focus on making sure that each stroke my feet take is at the right tempo and has enough power behind it. I'm not really one for meditation, but I think skating is probably the closest I get to being in a meditative state of mind. And I love it!

Sensory Expectations

For maximum safety whilst on eight wheels, you should be wearing a helmet and protective pads. Each of these places mild compression on the area of the body where they are worn, so it's important to make sure you choose kit that is comfortable. Otherwise, the pressure could become distracting and stop you from having fun. In terms of where to start learning to roller skate, sensory avoiders should beware of roller discos as they use bright flashing lights and loud music to create their party atmosphere. If your senses are easily over-stimulated, you would be better on a quiet residential road, cycle path or at a class.

Inline skates: plastic and PU leather upper, foam insoles and Velcro strap

Quad skates: PVC leather or leather upper, foam insoles and laces

Protective pads: elastic and Velcro straps, plastic shell and foam padding

Helmet: plastic shell, foam padding and nylon strap

Getting Started!

If you've got a pair of skates, a set of protective pads and a helmet, you're ready to roll! This kit can all be bought either new or second-hand online or at a local skate shop. If you're not the 'give it go and see what happens' type, there are plenty of great videos available online covering basic techniques that you can follow along with. Should you not have the kit or a nice smooth surface nearby to skate on, try a club or roller rink instead. A club can be anything from a local group of hobby skaters to classes run by a qualified coach. Roller rinks often offer quieter sessions in the early mornings for those who want to avoid the crowds, as well as discos in the evenings if you fancy a dance on your new wheels!

Support Recommendations

If you'd like to start a sport that doesn't call for much social interaction, roller skating could be for you. Recreational skating at a quiet spot local to your home is a great way to get active without having to interact with others. Whether learning on your own or with a coach, aim to keep each session simple. By practising just one or two movements or techniques whenever you head out to skate, you'll be minimizing your risk of overwhelm and giving your confidence the best chance to grow over time.

PROFILE
Name: Allie Mason
Country: England
Activity: Roller skating

How did you first get started with roller skating?
I used to pootle around our housing estate as a child on my roller skates and even have a photograph with my granddad from when I was around three years old on my first ever pair! So, I had experience with the sport from a very young age but didn't begin taking it seriously until

I was much older. It wasn't until I bought my first pair as an adult in 2020 that roller skating began to change my life. That sounds dramatic, but it's true – without my return to roller skating, I don't think I'd be sitting here writing this book!

What are the benefits that you have found from roller skating?
One of the greatest benefits for me has been the increase in my self-confidence. As you will know from reading the introductory section, 'My Story', sport has never been my strong point, and I struggled as a younger person to find a way to keep fit that was sustainable for me (I wish I'd realized when I was a child that roller skating was the answer!). Since making this sport a staple part of my weekly routine, I now look forward to beating my personal bests in distance or speed, and appreciate the boost to my wellbeing that a session on my wheels provides.

What are the main sensory issues, if any, that you face whilst roller skating?
For me, roller skating mostly leads to positive sensory experiences. It is an activity that stimulates your sense of balance through movement, such as changing direction or speed and being on wheels. I really enjoy how slow and rhythmic skating in one direction can have a calming effect on me, whilst fast skating with lots of turns gets my heart racing in excitement! I like being able to choose between the two approaches, depending on my sensory needs for that day.

How has being autistic impacted you (positively and/or negatively) in this activity?
I would say that I have struggled to learn things like the right posture or stroke technique due to my autistic brain. My coach will often give me tips on how to improve as I'm skating around the track, which I find difficult to process because I'm already concentrating on not falling flat on my face. However, once I

know how something feels in my body, I find it much easier to replicate. Verbal instructions can only get me so far, but after getting a technique right and recognizing how my body feels whilst doing it, I usually improve very quickly.

What advice would you give to an autistic young person who is interested in starting roller skating?
Learn the basics first: how to balance and how to fall. Once you are confident with those, it will feel a lot simpler to learn other techniques, as you will have a solid foundation to build on. I am only just becoming proficient in them now, two years after my return to roller skating! I am having to unlearn bad habits that I picked up from not prioritizing the basics, which is a really challenging process, and best avoided if you can help it.

RUNNING

Introduction

As you may well have expected, running was of course a 'thing' even before it became an official sport. To begin with, running was a purely functional activity, a way to quickly find food or evade danger for our ancestors. This changed, however, in Ancient Greece in 776 BCE, with the founding of the Olympic Games. For several decades afterwards, running was the only sport at this event, with the Greeks transforming this functional activity into a competitive one. The inclusion of marathon-length distances came later on, which leads us to the unearthing of a rather interesting fact. Whilst the cheetah, as the fastest land animal, can outrun a human in terms of speed, we humans can outrun a cheetah when it comes to longer distances like the marathon.

Why Try It?

If the thought of being physically capable of outrunning a cheetah isn't enough to get you interested, there are plenty of positives associated with this sport that might convince you to give it a go. In the first instance, running is an accessible activity that does not need you to have perfected specific techniques or to have understood a particular set of rules before you can get involved. It has also been proven as a way to reduce anxiety whilst increasing self-confidence and your personal sense of wellbeing. Those sound like pretty strong selling points to me! Plus, running is arguably the ideal match for the autistic brain, because improvement in this sport comes from consistency and repetition.

Sensory Expectations

The five main senses can all have a positive influence on the experience of the runner. As you start out, focusing on each of the senses, one at a time, can be used as a conscious method of distraction from tired legs or an inner voice of doubt. With sight, you could choose a few landmarks along the route to serve as sub-goals to celebrate. For smell, paying attention to the scents around you can help to acclimatize you to your surroundings more quickly. Taste is especially useful during a run, as the taste of salt in your mouth indicates dehydration, meaning you need to drink some water. With hearing, you could choose to focus on one particular noise and imagine where it is coming from, who is making it and how they got to your location. (A word of warning: if you're the type who can't stand unanswered questions, this probably isn't the approach for you – otherwise your run might come to an abrupt end as you decide to start looking for the real source of the noise instead!) For touch, it can be beneficial to concentrate on how the ground feels beneath your feet, particularly if your route takes you across multiple types of surfaces such as grass, mud, paving, sand or stones.

Leggings: polyester/ elastane mix

Top: polyester

Trainers: mesh upper with laces and rubber sole

Shorts: polyester

Getting Started!

Trainers with a grippy rubber sole? Check. Comfortable clothes that give you freedom to move? Check. With those two things sorted, you're ready to start running. Once you're kitted out, the next step is to select your running route. I'd recommend a circular course, whether that be at a local park, around the streets where you live or even laps of your garden, if it's on the bigger side! There's no pressure on you to be able to run the whole way to begin with either. A steady pace with intermittent walking breaks is ideal. Just make sure that, if you are going out alone, you let a friend or family member know where you'll be going. That way, if you decide that you've had enough or sustain an injury, there's someone ready to come and pick you up who knows where to find you.

Support Recommendations

An alternative to going running alone would be to bring that friend or family member along for support. Depending on your route, they could run or cycle beside you to help with navigation or simply to provide encouragement. The wider running community is often described as welcoming and inclusive, where what matters is the effort that you invest rather than the speed that you reach. It might therefore be worth considering joining a running club, with many local areas having clubs that specifically cater to autistic young people. This would be a very supportive environment, as the coaches will have had training and experience working with autistic athletes. A final recommendation comes from American runner Tommy Des Brisay. Tommy is well known for singing songs or reciting lines from his favourite films as he runs, helping him to concentrate and levelling up his enjoyment of every outing. Why not give it a try?

PROFILE

Name: Ashley Daniels
Country: United States of America
Activity: Running

How did you first get started with running?

I first got into this sport after casually running a couple of marathons that I hadn't trained for. I didn't think I'd be into it as much as I was because I was diagnosed with asthma and running was really hard. After I worked with a coach, I found that running had become a special interest. I wanted to know everything about it; I started coaching and got my certification to be a coach, all so I could know the ins and outs of the sport. I then joined a wonderful running community that I've been running with for four seasons, and they are my second family.

What are the benefits that you have found from running?

Running is a huge part of how I emotionally process my feelings. I'm happiest when I'm running and it is my greatest happy stim. After finding out that I'm autistic almost two years ago, I realized that throughout my life I used athletics in a sensory seeking way. I love moving my body and the dopamine and serotonin that comes with it.

In addition, running has allowed me to lean into my rigid thinking to use it to my advantage. Having a structured running plan is most helpful, alongside a strength training programme. It's how I've been able to improve my times so much in the last two seasons!

What are the main sensory issues, if any, that you face whilst running?

There are a lot of sensory issues that I experience while I'm running. Dehydration, forgetting to eat, high amounts of stress on the body, pushing my body too hard, if I wear the wrong shirt and the fabric catches on my skin, forgetting deodorant and the chafing that comes with that, running in the rain and the feeling of soggy socks, if my shoes are not tied the same way and they are too tight on my feet as a result, the loud noises of the city, WIND, sirens coming from emergency vehicles...just to name a few!

How has being autistic impacted you (positively and/or negatively) in this activity?

Along with my autism, I experience non-epileptic seizures and my seizures can be caused from over-stimulation, under-stimulation, stress, dehydration, forgetting to eat, etc. If I am not careful, I can collapse and have seizures, and it's happened multiple times while running.

Positively, I would not be as disciplined, determined, persistent and gritty if I wasn't autistic. Running would not be as deep of a passion as it is for me if it wasn't my special interest. I would not be on the brink of finally qualifying for the Boston Marathon without all of the qualities that I have listed above. Running truly is where I am happiest, and it encourages me to push myself in ways that I love.

What advice would you give to an autistic young person who is interested in starting running?

Start. Lace up your shoes and run down the block. But also, BE PATIENT! Running is an incredibly tough sport that requires patience, discipline and grit. If you stick with it, running is the greatest gift, and it also brings so many people together.

Join a running community. For me, I struggle with socializing, and joining a running community is something that has really pushed me out of my comfort zone, to make friends and find a place I feel like I belong. We may have to work twice as hard as our neurotypical and allistic counterparts, but we are not lesser than them because of it.

SAILING

Introduction

Sailing has been a mode of transportation in human society since ancient times, but it wasn't until the 17th century in Holland that it became something people did for sport. The City of Amsterdam actually bought a yacht, HMY Mary, to gift to King Charles II of England, which initiated the growth in popularity of recreational sailing across the world. Over two centuries later, in 1896, sailing was included in the Olympics for the very first time, in Athens. Unfortunately for the athletes, the weather that year was so bad that the sailing races couldn't be held and they had to wait until the 1900 Olympic Games in Paris to compete.

Why Try It?

The list of skills and abilities that are honed as a result of taking up sailing as a hobby is rather impressive: strength, endurance, flexibility, agility, balance, coordination, risk management and decision-making, to name only a few! If that's not enough to convince you that it's worth having a go, I'm not sure what would. As with many, if not all, of the other active pursuits in this book, sailing also helps to develop a greater understanding of our interconnectedness within the world, and enables you to explore a whole new environment.

Sensory Expectations

There are some obvious sensory expectations to have when participating in this sport, such as the noise created by the flapping sails and engine of the boat. In addition, however, there are some less obvious ones as well. For those who struggle with balance, sailing could present a challenge when it comes to retaining the right posture and controlling your movements on the boat.

For anyone like me who has difficulties with body awareness, avoiding obstacles on the boat could be a bit tricky! (It's also worth looking at the sensory expectation sections on the other water sports in these pages, like canoeing.)

Sailing gloves: synthetic leather or neoprene

Buoyancy aid: nylon outer shell, PVC padding, elasticated sides and nylon straps

Getting Started!

In case you were wondering, this is not going to be one of the sports where you can 100% teach yourself from a video! You'll want to go along to a local club for a taster session if you can, before signing up to sailing lessons if it's something you decide that you want to pursue. These will be taught by an experienced sailor or qualified instructor, where all the necessary equipment (from buoyancy aid to boat) will be provided for you. All you'll need to do is show up in clothes and shoes that you don't mind getting a bit wet.

Support Recommendations

There are many ways that an instructor can best support you as you are learning to sail, so it would be worth communicating any additional needs that you have before lessons start. One suggestion is to ask for safe places for you to stand on the boat to be marked with coloured tape, so that they are easy for you to remember. Another is to request extra time to get used to the sailing kit and boat before you begin your lessons, whether that be arriving early on the day or having the opportunity to familiarize yourself with these a few days in advance.

WHERE IN THE WORLD?

In the waters of the Zanzibar archipelago in East Africa, there is a sailing event that even the organizers describe as 'possibly the most ridiculous ocean race in the world'. In a boat crafted from the hollowed-out trunk of a mango tree, crews of three race one another in the Kraken Cup, an event that takes place over seven days and covers 180 miles. The boats are called Ngalawa and are almost identical to the traditional Tanzanian fishing boats of the same name still used in the region today. Sailors must make it to land before nightfall each evening, where they sleep on the sand, in a makeshift hammock or (for the lucky ones) as a guest in the house of a local family, before getting up the next day to do it all over again.

SKATEBOARDING

Introduction

The first skateboard was nothing more than a crate of wood with roller derby skates attached to the underside, which then evolved into a wooden pallet with clay wheels by the 1950s. You couldn't buy a skateboard from a shop until 1959, so the earliest skaters made their own. Almost two decades later, in 1976, the first skate park was built in Florida in the USA. Fast-forward again to the 1990s, and the rising popularity of punk and hip-hop also led to increased interest in skateboarding, where the sport began to take on the identity of a cultural movement as well as simply a way to stay active. A key moment in the history of skateboarding came in 1995 with the founding of the X Games, an event that brought together extreme sports from all across the globe.

Why Try It?

That cultural movement that I mentioned around skateboarding is one that places value on creativity, individuality and freedom. In the 21st century, it continues to be seen as a way of life that invites you to take risks in the pursuit of self-expression. Skaters don't try and compare themselves to one another, but instead encourage each other to aim for their full potential. You will find them coming together in the streets or taking to empty car parks to experiment on their boards and celebrate their collective achievements.

Sensory Expectations

You might not have realized before now but shoes are very

important to the experience of a skater. Your shoes need to enable you to feel the board beneath your feet in order to control it, so no heels or thick soles. These would prevent you from having the close contact with the board that you require. Just like with roller skating, you're going to want to wear protective pads, which place mild compression on the area of the body that they are worn on. Make sure your set is comfortable so that you aren't distracted by the pressure as you're trying to skateboard. This sport really is all about how your body feels as you're doing it, meaning your senses will be focused on the positioning of your feet, the bend in your knees and your overall posture.

Skateboard: wooden deck and plastic wheels

Helmet: plastic shell, foam padding and nylon strap

Protective pads: elastic and Velcro straps, plastic shell and foam padding

Getting Started!

Once you have your skateboard and set of protective pads – which can be bought either new or second-hand online or at a local skate shop – it's time to find a patch of grass to get practising on. At this stage you don't want the skateboard to be able to move, hence the grass! Practise leaning forward and backward using your toes and heels to get a feel for the board, remembering to bend your knees a little for stability. This is also a great way to identify which foot you prefer to have in front. Something else to remember, that you can start practising even while stationary, is to face the direction that you'd want to be moving in, as this will help maintain your momentum once you do get moving. When you are comfortable with the board, you can progress to a smooth surface and roll away!

Support Recommendations

Whilst on the grass it would be a good idea to also practise falling, because this gets you familiar with how the board will respond to this movement and how you should react. That way, when you progress to actual skateboarding, you won't be nervous or tense as you'll be confident in your ability to fall safely. If and when you're ready to go to a skate park, you'll have the best chance of finding it empty earlier in the morning, if the idea of socializing with other skaters is not your thing. Equally, you might want to try an empty car park instead, after the shops have closed, as a quiet alternative. As has been mentioned with previous activities, if you're heading out alone, make sure to let a parent or guardian know where you are going.

PROFILE
Name: Emily K
Country: England
Activity: Skateboarding

How did you first get started with skateboarding?
I always thought that skateboarding looked cool, and can specifically remember when my uncle

first gave me an old skateboard of his to try out. I'd push it back and forth across our garden patio (very bumpy!) and then upgraded to practising outside the front of my house as a child. I grew up continuing to enjoy skateboarding and progressed to skateboarding around the block of houses we lived near, as well as at my local park. I remember always getting so excited when I came across a super-smooth bit of new pavement to practise on!

What are the benefits that you have found from skateboarding?
A big benefit is the real sense of freedom that comes with just going out and finding the perfect spot, and then the continuous rhythm of pushing yourself along on a board. You can go wherever you like when you like. I enjoy the element of speed as well. It's something I've been able to build up over the years and ultimately get more comfortable with. That's another benefit, I think, in that it's challenging and there is always room to improve. I also think my balance has definitely improved the more that I have skateboarded, and I really like the feedback that a skateboard gives under both my feet. Being able to feel the direction I am going in when leaning into corners is just super-satisfying to me.

What are the main sensory issues, if any, that you face whilst skateboarding?
My foot feeling right on the board and pushing off correctly is a big one for me (something I used to struggle with as a child when learning to ride a bike, too, and definitely a tactile sensory issue). I have to push off the ground in a certain way and swivel onto the board the same each time, otherwise I have to start again as it doesn't feel right.

Another sensory issue I have is that it is difficult being out and about, as you never know what you might encounter in terms of things like overwhelming sights, sounds, smells, etc. It's hard to prepare for, but I find it can be helpful to take supports such as ear defenders and a fidget toy with me.

Also, the weather! It can be very disruptive in general, but sensory-wise, it's frustrating too.

How has being autistic impacted you (positively and/or negatively) in this activity?
I think a positive thing is that skateboarding gets me out of the house and can be quite a social sport. On our annual family holiday to Cornwall in the UK, I like to skateboard with my sister, and we always pack our boards to take with us. It's something we enjoy doing together, and we chat about so many things as we coast along!

A negative aspect is that the wayfinding and navigational element is tricky for me. I tend to do the same loops or stretches of road when skateboarding, back and forth. I like the rhythm and familiarity, and that way I don't go too far or get lost. I don't really venture past certain areas unless I am with someone else.

What advice would you give to an autistic young person who is interested in starting skateboarding?
My top tips:

- Start by working out the position of your feet. There are two types of stances in skateboarding: regular and goofy. Goofy means that you skate with your right foot at the front of the board and push along the ground with your left foot. Regular means that you skate with your left foot at the front of the board and push along the ground with your right foot. You'll work it out by what feels more natural to you (as one will feel odd and totally unnatural!)
- If you can, why not try and borrow a board from someone

you know, or hire one for a day? That way you can see if it is something you might like without having to invest too much.

- If you would like to buy a skateboard yourself, have a look around at all the different types, and do some research through reading reviews and watching comparison videos (boards come in a range of sizes, shapes and styles). It's really exciting to pick out a cool colour and style of board, so have fun with it.
- It's important to always ride with a helmet, no matter how experienced you are. If you can buy padded elbow and knee pads, they are really worth it, especially when first starting out, to protect yourself from bumps and grazes. You can also wear a long-sleeve top and full-length trousers for added protection.
- I recommend taking a backpack if you are skateboarding further afield, with either sun or rain essentials inside, depending on whereabouts you live. Also, it's always a good idea to take your phone with you if you are going out alone, and to let a friend or family member know where you are going and what time to expect you back.
- Try practising near a railing when first starting out. It can be super-helpful to lean on and guide yourself along with (and gives you something to grab onto if the skateboard whips out from underneath you suddenly!).
- Avoid skateboarding in busy places and near roads as it can be quite disorientating, distracting and not very safe.
- If you want to get into tricks, it's a good idea to practise near grass so you have the option of a softer landing. There are lots of great tutorials online for beginners. I recommend starting out by learning how to Ollie, as it's a core skill to have that you can build other tricks from.
- Don't get disheartened if it's super-tricky to start with! It's a cliché, but I promise, practice makes perfect. The more you get outside and on your board, the better you'll become.

SKIING

Introduction

It is estimated that the first person to attach two sticks to their feet for the purpose of better transportation lived over 20,000 years ago. This method of travel came about as a way in the winter to cross frozen marshes and wetlands. There are even cave drawings depicting prehistoric skiing dating from the end of the last Ice Age. Fast-forward to the 20th century, and skiing completed the transition into a recreational activity with the invention of the chairlift by an American engineer. Now, people can easily ride up a mountain just for the chance to ski back down it.

Why Try It?

Skiing is a wonderful hobby to pick up at any age, albeit an expensive one. It is that perfect combination of a sport that is social, yet not team-based, where you can enjoy sharing the experience with others without the additional challenges that teamwork can invoke for us autistic folk. It's also the right kind of environment to learn how to fail whilst having fun! Falling over during a ski session just means risking a mouthful of snow, but 'failing' in this way is a valuable transferable skill for other areas of your life too.

Sensory Expectations

SNOW. I feel like I can leave it at that, but I won't. Being around snow, especially for extended periods of time, will probably lead to a bit of sensory overwhelm for the following reasons. The glare of the sun off the snow tires the eyes, whilst the uneven surface of it beneath your feet will challenge your sense of balance. As a beginner who will be falling a lot (there's no shame, that's how everyone starts!), the snow will be cold and wet against your skin. On the positive side, as it is made up of water, is not likely to really smell or taste of anything if you do get a face full.

Gloves: polyester with elasticated cuffs and rayon lining

Goggles: plastic frame with elastic strap

Helmet: plastic shell with foam padding, fleece lining and nylon strap

Jacket: polyester with down lining

Salopettes: polyester with fleece lining and elasticated waistband

Getting Started!

It seems like a super-young age to me, but apparently the majority of ski schools will accept students from the age of four or five, so if you're reading this, you're definitely old enough to start having lessons! This is recommended as the best way to learn as a qualified instructor can support you to learn the basics in a relatively short period of time. If you don't live near a snowy mountain range, fear not. There are other options such as dry slopes or indoor centres available in most countries. In any of these locations it should be possible to hire skis, boots and a helmet.

You will then need to bring goggles, gloves, salopettes and a ski jacket to wear.

Support Recommendations

When planning your ski lessons, bear in mind the time of year and location that you have chosen, as school holidays and popular resorts are sure to be crowded on the slopes. I personally have been learning to ski on a local dry slope, where numbers are limited and the earlier sessions are quieter. If you have bought your ski gear – as opposed to hiring it when you get there – take the opportunity to try it on in advance, to familiarize yourself with how it sits against your body. Finally, when you are at the lesson itself, from experience I'd suggest always asking the instructor to show rather than tell you what to do. I find it much easier to mimic someone's posture than try to create it myself from verbal instructions, as an example.

PROFILE
Name: Alice Willans
Country: England
Activity: Skiing

How did you first get started with skiing?
When I was a child, I went on three skiing holidays with my dad and sister. I enjoyed them and I picked up skiing without much difficulty. I really enjoyed skiing, and it was brilliant exploring snowy mountains.

In September 2018, when I was 19 years old, I joined Aldershot Skiing for the Disabled (ASD) because I wanted to get back into skiing, have the opportunity to go skiing abroad with a group and be part of a skiing club. After skiing there for a few months with a guide on the nursery slope, my progress was back to where it was when I had last been skiing five years before. I tried the slalom course on the main slope and really enjoyed it. I was then asked if I wanted to join the Special Olympics Surrey ski race team (who are part of ASD). I had never heard of the Special Olympics before but I was very excited, because I have always wanted to be an athlete, and this was my chance!

What are the benefits that you have found from skiing?
Skiing is more than a sport to me, as it has given me the opportunity to meet new friends through training and competing as a team. In February 2020, the majority of my team and I competed at the Special Olympics Great Britain National Alpine skiing competition in Crans-Montana, Switzerland. This was one of the best experiences of my life so far, because I really enjoyed it and it was the first time I was proud to be a part of something since leaving my specialist school in 2015. We are a very diverse and supportive group and we all have a range of different support needs. However, we all support each other in our own ways and socialize as a group. I also had the opportunity to become friends with other skiers in different teams across Great Britain. At the Nationals for the first time, I made really good friends with an autistic girl who is a year older than me. We have similar interests and we just clicked, but we would never have met if it wasn't for skiing and the Special Olympics. One of the reasons I felt isolated before I started ski racing was because I only had one female friend. Then, having another female friend who I shared the passion for skiing with was brilliant for both of us.

Skiing also improves my fitness and allows me to be outside, which is particularly useful as it helps me manage my type 1 diabetes. Skiing gives me a focus and structure, something to work towards and be a part of outside of studying my horticulture course at college. I am at my happiest when I'm outdoors and being active.

What are the main sensory issues, if any, that you face whilst skiing?

I would say for me skiing provides lots of positive sensory input. It is normally quiet on the slopes, because everyone is focusing on their skiing. I find the views and scenery absolutely stunning. The best sensory input that skiing gives me is when I am skiing down the racecourse. I get a massive adrenaline rush and I feel super-focused. My mind is only thinking about going around the red and blue gates and going as fast as I possibly can, whilst feeling in control. I also like hearing everyone cheering me on in the background because it makes me feel supported and proud.

There are sensory challenges that may come with skiing, but most can be overcome. I did find my first skiing trip stressful and I did face some challenges. My main sensory challenge was my ski boots as they feel tight and uncomfortable; however, this can be the case for most people. I struggle with walking in my ski boots whilst carrying my skis, especially in the gondola queue, but I know this is the only way up the mountain. I am able to put these struggles to one side as I am resilient and I know this is just a part of skiing.

How has being autistic impacted you (positively and/or negatively) in this activity?

Being autistic has positively impacted me in skiing because I have had the opportunity to be part of a disability skiing group and the Special Olympics, where I have met like-minded people but also had the chance to race in competitions. However, I found ski school abroad quite challenging because it takes me longer than my mainstream peers to learn a new skill and process verbal information.

I had a positive experience of ski school on my last skiing holiday. The group I was in suited me much better because the other children in the group were much younger than me. This worked very well because it took away all of the pressure and anxiety of trying to communicate and be as good as other skiers of my own age. They were all German or Austrian children and I was the only English child in the group; however, they were all very friendly to me and I was able to keep up and even help the others when they fell over, which boosted my confidence.

What advice would you give to an autistic young person who is interested in starting skiing?
In the UK, most areas have a disability snow sports club, so I would advise that autistic children and young people should do some research on their local ski clubs to see what they offer. (If you don't live in the UK, this might be the same in your country too.) A disability or adaptive ski club is ideal for an autistic child or young person as it is a calmer and supportive environment, because everyone there understands autism a little bit better. Opportunities may arise from being part of the club, and you can test out whether you enjoy skiing before going abroad. You may even want to become part of a Special Olympics race team! If you were to go abroad, it might be worth having an instructor who is aware of autism so that your specific circumstances can be taken into consideration. It might be a good idea to have smaller classes or private lessons abroad, as well as a ski instructor who speaks your own language.

SLACKLINING

Introduction

You might not have guessed this but slacklining
– the act of balancing on tensioned webbing –
emerged out of the climbing community
(specifically in Yosemite National Park in the
early 1980s) rather than from the circus scene and
tightrope walking, as you might have expected.
The popularity of this sport began to skyrocket in
the mid-2000s after simple at-home kits came
onto the European market. A slackline kit is made
up of a length of webbing and a tensioning system,
as well as two tree slings and a pair of tree
protectors. What have trees got to do with it, I
hear you ask? Well, in order for you to balance
on and walk along the aforementioned
webbing, it needs to be firmly secured between two fixed points.
Trees are rather useful for that exact purpose.

Why Try It?

It should almost go without saying that the first reason you should
try slacklining is because it's insanely cool. How many people
do you know who can perform tricks on a 2–5 cm wide length
of webbing? Not many, I'd bet. As well as giving yourself a nice
confidence boost by being great at something unusual, this sport
is a safe way to improve your balance, agility and concentration.
After all, the slackline itself will be rigged low to the ground,
meaning there won't be too far to fall if you do have a wobble.

To succeed, you'll need to begin by taking slow and controlled steps, which is where the concentration aspect is especially crucial. Over time, as you get more comfortable, you can progress to learning tricks.

Sensory Expectations

If you are interested in exploring the effects of gravity on your body and its movements, this is the hobby for you. For anyone whose systems of balance and body awareness are over-sensitive, slacklining offers a route to positive and rewarding stimulation of those systems. From working on your balance to performing the kind of tricks you would normally see on a trampoline, the journey towards proficiency will stimulate your senses every step of the way (yup, another pun!). Once on the slackline, if you find that you would rather have a bit more grip beneath your feet, it is possible to find webbing with rubberized print to help.

Getting Started!

That basic slackline kit outlined earlier is all you need to get started. If you're lucky enough to have two trees in your back garden of at least 60 cm in circumference each, spaced 5 to 10 metres apart, then you don't even have to leave the comfort of your own home. Otherwise, you'll want to head down to your local park. Make sure to use tree protectors or something like a car floor mat to prevent damage to the bark. You want your slackline to be set up just below knee height, in order to safely manage any falls. If, like me, you're not the biggest fan of grass against your skin, lay down some blankets or an old sheet first. Oh, and check for stones, too! You'd be feeling pretty miserable – and bruised – if you fell on a pointy rock. When you're standing on the slackline, raise your arms above your head, keep both your toe and heel on the line and focus your eyes on something unmoving in front of you.

Support Recommendations

Something that I learned from roller skating that equally applies here is that it is very important to be comfortable with falling. Otherwise, you'll be so scared of what might happen if you do that you won't be able to concentrate properly. Build your confidence by practising purposefully stepping down from the line. Further ways to support yourself as you start out include rigging a helpline above your head to hold onto or asking a friend or family member to hold your hand/s at first. If you have walking poles lying around from hikes or even just find some long branches at the park, you could hold one end and rest the other on the ground whilst you get used to the feeling of standing on the line.

WHERE IN THE WORLD?

Before I tell you more about this epic achievement, I want to make it very clear that I do not recommend trying this at home. In April 2020 on the archipelago of Vanuatu in the South Pacific Ocean, two extreme athletes rigged their 260-metre slackline across the crater of the active volcano Mount Yasur. The lava was 900°C, with shock waves from the continuous eruptions that would throw the athletes off their line. The two men wore protective masks because of the sulphuric gases as they crossed, dodging lava bombs along the way. It took years of research for them to locate an active volcano that was suitable for the stunt. If you want to watch the nail-biting footage for yourself, just search online for 'LavaLine World Record'.

SNORKELLING

Introduction

Legend has it that the idea for the snorkel came to the Greek philosopher Aristotle as he watched an elephant using its trunk to breathe underwater back in the 4th century. However, predecessors to the snorkel were being used for centuries beforehand, such as the way that the Assyrian people in around 900 BCE were filling animal skins with air to dive with, in order to spend longer underwater without having to come up to the surface to breathe. Nowadays snorkels are made from more durable materials in order to withstand the corrosion from salt water and remain usable for a number of years after their manufacture.

Why Try It?

Snorkelling is a more affordable and more flexible alternative to scuba diving when it comes to getting up close with marine wildlife and habitats. The fact that snorkellers don't produce bubbles as they explore makes them appear less threatening to sea creatures, who are less likely to hide or swim away if they see you coming than if you were a diver. This activity is a great option for those who wish to experience underwater environments without causing any harm whilst doing so. The mantra to remember as you swim beneath the waves is: don't disturb the ecosystem, don't draw attention to yourself and don't try to feed those curious sea creatures!

Sensory Expectations

Getting used to breathing through a snorkel is going to be the most challenging aspect by far of this activity. You have to breathe through your mouth only, which, for anyone like me, who naturally breathes through their nose, is going to feel very strange indeed. The best approach to this would be to practise well before you reach the sea, either in your local swimming pool or even in your bath at home. If you find that you struggle with maintaining your balance whilst floating why not take an inflatable along with you? That way you can relax and enjoy the experience without worrying about staying afloat.

Snorkel fins: rubber

Snorkel: glass lens, plastic frame and silicone skirt

Snorkel mask: glass lens, plastic frame and silicone skirt

Swimsuit: nylon

Getting Started!

To be safe in the water, best practice is to make sure that you are a confident swimmer before you try snorkelling for the first time. Much like with the snorkel itself, you'll probably want to have a go at swimming with your fins in a familiar environment ahead of your trip, as the extra weight and drag takes a little time to adapt to comfortably. Once these steps are complete, you're ready for the sea! When you are swimming amongst the waves and looking down on all the marvellous marine sights, try to relax and let your fins do the hard work rather than pulling yourself through the water with your arms. Stay alert to the strength of the current and don't let it sweep you off somewhere that you don't want to go!

Support Recommendations

It's really important that you put in the practice before snorkelling in the sea itself, so that you fully understand how to use the snorkel and fins before immersing yourself in a strange new underwater world. When choosing the right location on the coastline, find somewhere that you can still reach the sea floor to stand up if you need to. Not only does this make it easy to rest if you start to feel tired, but it also provides you with peace of mind that you can always walk back to shore. For your safety, especially if you're inclined to hyperfocus or if there is the risk of strong currents in your chosen location, ask someone to stay close by so that they can look out for you whilst you snorkel.

ALLIE'S FIRST ATTEMPT

I know that I was definitely taken snorkelling as a child, but I can't remember anything about the experience. However, I do remember going snorkelling in the Seychelles when I was visiting a friend there in 2018. She was volunteering on a turtle conservation project. She took me to a sandy cove that was peppered with huge boulders and had the kind of stunningly turquoise sea that you usually only find on postcards. I started by sitting on the beach and letting the waves wash over me, to get used to the change of dry to wet skin. Then I snorkelled in the shallows, with water so clear that I could see the sunlight dappling the seabed and little fish swimming all around me. As you know by now, I'm not usually one for swimming, but this is an amazing memory and an experience I'm really grateful to have had.

SNOWBOARDING

Introduction

I don't know about you, but I'm very disappointed that snowboards are no longer called 'snurfers', like they were when they were first invented in 1965. By the end of the 1970s, sales of the snurfer had reached 1 million, illustrating the sport's stratospheric growth in its early years. The interest of the skateboarding community was piqued in the 1980s, which makes sense when you reflect on how similar a snowboard looks to an oversized skateboard without wheels. Since then, this sport has only continued to grow in popularity.

Why Try It?

Snowboarding has expanded to encompass three different disciplines, each with a different pace and style. It's therefore a great sport to get into due to the range of ways that you can use your skills once you've learned how to ride. Not to mention that if you are already a skateboarder or surfer, or are interested in trying those activities, these skills will be transferable. First up is freestyle, where moves and tricks are performed in the air using either natural or man-made features of the slope. Next is freeriding, where the goal is simply to use the natural terrain to descend. Then we have alpine, which involves events like slalom and boardercross, where snowboarders compete against one another whilst using and/or avoiding obstacles.

Sensory Expectations

Definitely take a look at the section for skiing, where I explain some of the sensory inputs to expect from being surrounded by snow.

This is especially relevant to snowboarders, as they are unable to rest standing up by leaning on ski poles, meaning that they spend more time sitting or kneeling on the snow. The extra gear that you should wear for safety, including knee pads and wrist guards, add an additional sensory element to the experience. Much like with roller skating, you'd be best to take the time to find protective gear that is comfortable, so that the pressure of wearing it doesn't distract you on the slopes.

Gloves: polyester with elasticated cuffs and rayon lining

Goggles: plastic frame with elastic strap

Helmet: plastic shell with foam padding, fleece lining and nylon strap

Jacket: polyester with down lining

Trousers: polyester with fleece lining and elasticated waistband

Getting Started!

The same applies here as it did for skiing: lessons with a qualified instructor, whether at a mountain resort, indoor centre or a dry slope, are the best starting point. It's worth bearing in mind that the minimum age for a beginner is a little higher, however, at around seven or eight years old. As noted earlier, you'll need knee pads and wrist guards, as well as goggles, gloves and a snowboarding jacket and trousers. You can get gloves with built-in wrist guards if preferred. Snowboard trousers have extra padding compared to salopettes (due to the amount of time a snowboarder spends on their bum!).

Support Recommendations

With there being so many pieces of kit to remember, you might find it useful to make a checklist that you can go through before you leave home for your lesson, to ensure that you have everything you need. If you have your own snowboard or access to one before your lesson starts, take some time to get to know what the different parts of the board are called. When an instructor talks to you about the 'toe and heel edges' or refers to the 'tip' or 'tail' of the board, you'll feel a lot less under pressure if you focused on learning what these names mean ahead of even setting foot on the snow.

WHERE IN THE WORLD?

If heading to your local dry slope or to one of the more mainstream snowsport resorts isn't exciting enough for you, I've found some pretty spectacular spots where you can get your adrenaline kick instead. First up there's the Solang Valley in India, with its highest peak of 2560 metres, which forms part of the Pir Panjal mountain range. Why is this a cool spot to board? Well, because when you get too tired to hike back up to the top of the slope, you can only go and hire a **yak** to carry you up there. Second, there's Maunakea in Hawaii, the first-born child of the Earth Mother Papahānaumoku and Sky Father Wākea, according to native Hawaiian tradition. This 4205 metre dormant volcano looks like it should be a crater on the moon rather than a snowsport destination, with space observatories that you can visit on your way back.

Finally, I've saved the best until last: Mount Ruapehu on New Zealand's North Island. Why is it the best, you ask? Because it was a filming location for the *Lord of the Rings* trilogy, of course! Who wouldn't want to snowboard down the active volcano where Frodo and Sam once stood?

STAND UP PADDLEBOARDING

① ② ③

Introduction

It's difficult to say exactly how and when stand up paddleboarding first came to be, as it most likely developed simultaneously in different locations across the globe. We do know, however, that the oldest photographic record of this activity is from 1886, of a man stand up paddling through the English marshes of East Anglia. Its popularity grew once it was adopted by surfers who used stand up paddleboarding to reach quieter places to surf away from the crowds. Others soon realized that SUP, as it is often shortened to, could be a sport in its own right. That's how we have ended up with a strong community of both recreational and racing paddlers today.

Why Try It?

If you are somebody who already enjoys yoga and swimming, SUP might just be the perfect fit for you. It requires a combination of muscle strength and balance that you'll have already honed, whilst remaining an equally low impact form of keeping fit. If that isn't you, however, that doesn't mean you shouldn't go for a paddle yourself. SUP is very accessible and can even be done kneeling or sitting down (despite the name!) if you have reduced mobility.

Sensory Expectations

Standing on an unstable surface like a paddleboard is naturally going to take a little while to get used to, so it's worth being aware that you are more likely to fall into the water as you start learning than with other sports such as kayaking or canoeing. The most input is going to be to your senses of balance and body awareness. Don't despair if that means it takes you longer to master standing up on the board, and equally don't feel embarrassed if you have to kneel or sit down instead. In all honesty, I think that's what I would have to do, and I wouldn't mind one bit!

Gloves: neoprene

Buoyancy aid: nylon outer shell, PVC padding, elasticated sides and nylon straps

Boots: neoprene upper, rubber sole and Velcro straps

Wetsuit: neoprene

Getting Started!

I'd recommend finding a water sports club or activity centre local to you, where you can begin by learning both water safety and self-rescue techniques, as well as how to paddle the board. What you need to take with you will depend on the weather - sunscreen if it's sunny, a waterproof if it's raining, thermals to go under a wetsuit if it's cold. The benefit of going to a club or activity centre is that they will provide you with a buoyancy aid, in addition to a board and paddle. If it's sunny and you are going on the water in your own clothes, make sure to take a towel and a spare set of clothes for changing into once you're done.

Support Recommendations

As I mentioned earlier, the best thing to do if you are struggling to stay standing on your board is to kneel or sit instead. It may be called stand up paddleboarding, but that doesn't mean it can't be adapted for mobility or sensory needs. If it would be helpful, ask if you can mark the part of the board where you need to stand/kneel/sit with waterproof tape to help keep you in the right place, especially if you fall off and have to climb back on again.

PROFILE
Name: Layla Crehan
Country: United States of America
Activity: Stand up paddleboarding

How did you first get started with stand up paddleboarding?
The first sport that I ever got involved in – not only to help with anxiety, but also to stay fit – was swimming. I started competing on the Special Olympics swim team when I was 10. Once I was a really strong swimmer, I was then able to join other water sports (I compete in seven sports for the Special Olympics). When I was 12, I joined the Special Olympics Stand Up Paddleboarding team. I had a coach named Victoria who was a champion paddler and she inspired me to be the best that I could be. When I was 13, I sold my art to raise money to buy my own racing board and started ocean

racing! Since then, I have been ocean, lake and river racing all year long. The paddling community in the mainstream world is so amazing and inclusive. I have met people from all over the world, and they have been so kind and supportive on my journey. I still compete with the Special Olympics, but I have also competed and won gold medals in the 2020 Junior Olympics for Women 15 to 19 and the 2020 Sunshine State Games for Women 15 to 19. This past summer I attempted to cross the ocean from Bimini, Bahamas to Lake Worth, Florida, 80 miles, in the Crossing for Cystic Fibrosis. I was the youngest person to ever attempt it, and I really wanted to inspire other girls my age to set big goals and reach for their dreams! Due to rough conditions, I didn't make the full 80 miles on my first attempt, but I do intend to finish what I started. My goal was to be a part of the Crossing and inspire people while raising money for families with Cystic Fibrosis, and I reached my goal. My plan was to cross the 80 miles, but the sea had other plans for me.

What are the benefits that you have found from stand up paddleboarding?

Stand up paddleboarding makes me feel confident, strong and ready for anything. It helps a lot with my anxiety, because I love to be on the ocean and see lots of wildlife. I learned so much about fitness and nutrition and live a much healthier life now. I have made tons of friends and have gone on to learn so many new water sports, like surfing, open water swimming, kite surfing and outrigger canoeing!

What are the main sensory issues, if any, that you face whilst stand up paddleboarding?

The only sensory issue that I have experienced is having the sunlight in my eyes. If I don't wear dark sunglasses, I get a headache. Also, when the waves get really rough, like 3 to 6 feet (1 to 2 metres), sometimes I will get a stomach ache. But I spend a lot of time practising, preparing and training, and always finish what I start, no matter how tough it is. Sometimes my muscles will get sore, so I have learned to do certain yoga poses on my board to stretch my back, legs and shoulders. I have to have music in one ear all the time to keep me motivated and in the zone. The other ear is always open, to listen for danger.

How has being autistic impacted you (positively and/or negatively) in this activity?

My autism can give me a little trouble when it comes to anxiety. Sometimes my head will work against me. When I have set a big goal and it starts to get tough, my mind tells me I can't do it and I will get upset and sometimes even cry. So, I have to work really hard to keep positive thoughts in my head and to focus on the one main goal...finish! Sometimes people underestimate me because of my autism, but that just makes me fight harder and makes the win even sweeter. A positive thing that my autism has done for my sports is that I am very focused. When I start a race, all I see is the finish line, and it doesn't matter if it's 3 miles or 20 miles away. My mom calls it tunnel vision, and I think it is a gift!

What advice would you give to an autistic young person who is interested in starting stand up paddleboarding?

I would tell them they should be a strong swimmer. Safety first always! Next, be patient with yourself and allow yourself to make mistakes, because that's how we learn. Also, set small goals for yourself, such as short distances, and celebrate every victory. Don't ever let anyone tell you that you are not good enough or strong enough! You can do anything if you set your mind and heart to it. And most importantly, have fun!

STARGAZING

Introduction

The beauty of stargazing, I find, is in its simplicity. Whilst you can get invested in identifying all of the different constellations – and that's something we will get on to later in this section – for me, the simple act of gazing on the stars and marvelling at the sheer magnitude of the universe is a powerful enough experience. You can embark on a journey across time and space with nothing but your eyes

and your imagination. Even without a telescope, you will be able to see the distant planets of Mercury, Venus, Mars, Jupiter and Saturn, as well as the moon and our spectacular home galaxy of the Milky Way. If you live at the far reaches of either the northern or southern hemisphere, you could also be fortunate enough to witness the aurora borealis (Northern Lights) or the aurora australis (Southern Lights).

Why Try It?

Apart from the pure wonder of it all, there are other persuasive reasons to have a go at stargazing. You could, for instance, use it as an opportunity to start a moon journal, charting its phases across the lunar month and observing how it changes during that time. To do this, draw a picture of the moon in a notebook on every night that you see it, writing down the date and time next to each drawing. Another idea is to incorporate stargazing into your daily routine, where it can help you to identify the difference between night and day, as well as to understand when it is time to go to bed. I love this suggestion because it makes stargazing into an activity that you can look forward to doing every day.

Sensory Expectations

Depending on whereabouts in the world you live and what time of year it is, chances are that it's going to get cold being outside late in the evening. Should you not mind the colder temperatures and decide to brave the outside after dark, you'll want to wrap up warm in layers of clothing that will trap your body heat. If, however, you find those colder temperatures more difficult to deal with, you can always try stargazing from an upstairs window with the lights turned off instead. The one sensory input that you can definitely count on being present, though, is light. I bet you guessed that already! Steady lights that move across the night sky as you watch them are spacecraft orbiting the Earth, whilst unmoving steady lights are one of the other planets in our galaxy. Twinkling lights are the actual stars and fast streaks of light that disappear after a few seconds are meteors. If you are particularly sensitive to light, it might be best to do your stargazing sessions little and often, rather than stay out on one particular evening for an extended period of time.

Getting Started!

For your first, and indeed every, stargazing session, you want to choose an evening with a clear sky, as clouds will obstruct your view. Heading outside? Make sure to wrap up warm. Staying inside? Don't forget to turn off all of the lights in that room. For a more scientific approach, you can prepare to have some resources in advance that will help you to identify exactly what you can see.

Skymaps.com has free printable downloads showing where the constellations are local to you, whilst a planetarium app like Star Chart enables you to plot the positions of planets and stars by holding a mobile phone up to the night sky.

Support Recommendations

At first, it can feel very disorienting whilst your eyes try to adjust to the darkness. It's recommended that, at the beginning of your stargazing, you close your eyes and count to 20. Afterwards, when you open your eyes again, they will be ready for the darkness. If you require extra physical support when reclining your head back to look upwards at the night sky, you could lie on something like a sun lounger, which would provide support for your entire upper body. Alternatively, on warm and dry evenings, you could lie on the ground with a cushion or pillow behind your head.

ALLIE'S FIRST ATTEMPT

I was very fortunate to grow up in a rural market town in the Yorkshire Dales where there was a reasonably low level of light pollution, in comparison to big cities or more built-up areas. This meant that whenever I came home after dark, I would always take a moment to stop and marvel at the starlit sky above me. I've never been one for trying to identify the constellations. Instead, I prefer to use my time stargazing to wonder at how incredibly insignificant I am in the context of the vast universe that we live in. Whilst this might sound a bit disheartening at first, I am actually comforted and encouraged by this thought, because it reminds me that a lot of the things I might worry about (for example, what others think of me) don't matter that much at all.

SURFING

Introduction

I have a lot of respect for the first person who looked at a wave and thought, 'wouldn't it be cool if I could ride that all the way into the shore?' They must have been a brave soul! It's widely acknowledged that surfing as we know it today is descended from Polynesian tradition, brought back to a diverse array of homelands by the tourists who first began visiting Pacific Islands such as Hawaii in the early 1900s. Traditional surfboards were very heavy and very large, with the biggest reserved for the tribal chief as a sign of their power amongst the people.

Why Try It?

Have you ever heard of the 'blue mind' theory? It suggests that we, as humans, are naturally drawn to bodies of water, because they lead us into a meditative state of mind. Many surfers report feeling this way whilst riding a wave, as they develop a deep connection with the water and learn to anticipate what it will do before those actions are even visible. Aside from developing this connection, a further reason to try surfing is for the wealth of physical health benefits that it is known to provide. This sport improves balance and endurance, as well as facilitating a better sense of timing and better coordination skills.

Sensory Expectations

That 'blue mind' theory that I mentioned also makes sense when you think about the calming sensory inputs that water is known to produce. Feelings of weightlessness and the soothing rhythm of the waves have a positive effect on your sense of balance, while some surfers find that the body awareness challenges that they face on land don't seem to exist in the water. The one thing to keep in mind that might lead to sensory irritation is that you'll need to attach your surfboard to your ankle via a leash, to ensure it doesn't float away from you if you fall off during a wave.

Surfboard: foam or plastic

Swimsuit: nylon

Getting Started!

The one piece of kit that you 100% need to start surfing is a board, although many choose to wear wetsuits as well in order to stay warm in the water. It's best to begin with a longboard, as they are easier to paddle and more stable to balance on, so you'll want to either borrow or hire one of these at first. In the same way as snorkelling, start by practising using this kit away from the sea. It would be a good idea to practise 'popping up' at home or on the beach at first, which is when you jump up on the board from a horizontal position using your arms to push your body upright. When you're ready to hit the waves, choose somewhere that isn't overcrowded, ideally a sandy-bottomed area where the water is only chest or waist height deep.

Support Recommendations

It can be dangerous as a new starter, with a limited grasp of what to do and how to do it, to try and ride the same waves as the more experienced surfers. In fact, there is actually a lot of etiquette surrounding surfing. These unspoken rules – I know, an autistic person's worst nightmare! – are in place to ensure the safety of everyone on the water, regardless of experience level. I'd recommend that, when you are first learning to surf, you do so with a friend, family member or instructor who knows what they are doing already. That way, they can explain the etiquette to you and help you to understand the waves and tidal patterns. You'll then be having your own *Lilo & Stitch* moment before you know it.

PROFILE

Name: Cassidy Nicholas
Country: United States of America
Activity: Surfing

How did you first get started with surfing?

I started surfing when I was about six or seven years old, being pushed into waves by my parents. My parents were into boating, so, once I got my driver's licence at 16, I was able to surf more often. It wasn't until I was 26 years old that I got my first longboard and was able to surf more regularly. I then improved more in a few months than I had in years.

What are the benefits that you have found from surfing?

Being in the ocean is my happy place. I get to see dolphins, manta rays, sea turtles and other smiling surfers. I love being able to get all of my energy out and express myself on a wave. I love yelling and cheering for myself and others. I feel like I can truly unmask. I end some waves with a front or back flip off my board. When waiting for waves, I allow myself to stim and feel all the energy that the ocean has. The ocean is my playground, and surfing allows me to feel that autistic joy uninhibited.

What are the main sensory issues, if any, that you face whilst surfing?

My hair gets very dry and tangled. My skin gets bumps, bruises and burns. I try to wear my hair in braids if I can, to help with the tangles, and I bring leave-in conditioner to put in my hair right after surfing. I have a jug of water, shampoo, soap, conditioner and extra clothes so that I can get the salt water off my skin as soon as possible.

How has being autistic impacted you (positively and/or negatively) in this activity?

The ocean is my favourite place to be myself. To unmask. I can stim while waiting for waves and I can't help but express that excitement while riding a wave. There is a lot of etiquette involved, which isn't obvious at first paddle out. Researching that etiquette in advance can help prevent miscommunications and potentially dangerous situations.

What advice would you give to an autistic young person who is interested in starting surfing?

Do your research! I pretty much taught myself everything I know from YouTube, but talking to locals and other people in the water gives you such an advantage too. Be a sponge. It's all about learning, improving and enjoying the ride.

TRIATHLON

Introduction

Triathlon is a unique entry in this book for the reason that it is a multi-sport activity, which includes swimming, cycling and running. These three activities are performed consecutively to create what we call the 'triathlon'. For an adult, the standard distances for each stage are a 1.5km swim, a 40km cycle and a 10km run. The International Triathlon Union, however, recognizes athletes as young as eight years old to participate. At that age the distances covered are necessarily shorter, with races consisting of a 100m swim, a 1.5km cycle and a 600m run.

Why Try It?

As with many of the active pursuits featured in these pages, the benefits of participating in the triathlon span both physical and mental wellbeing. For the former it will surely come as no surprise that triathletes build strength and endurance; however, you might not be aware that training in three sports (as opposed to just one) leads to less injuries associated with the overuse of specific muscle groups. For the latter, triathlon participants experience increases in their confidence, self-esteem and sense of independence.

Sensory Expectations

It is very likely that the biggest challenge for an autistic triathlete is going to be the transitions between each stage, especially the one between the swim and the cycle. For established participants the preferred kit is a trisuit, which they will wear throughout the entirety of the race. Whilst this removes the need to change outfit during the first transition, it does mean that you'll be cycling with the sensation of your trisuit drying against your skin. Another possible challenge is the changing weather, as the triathlon is a long race that could see you facing multiple elements along the route. If you know that you struggle with a particular type of weather, it would be worth intentionally choosing to train in it so that you can find effective solutions to any sensory issues before the race itself.

Goggles: plastic frame with silicone strap

Helmet: plastic shell, foam padding and nylon strap

Trainers: mesh upper with laces and rubber sole

Trisuit: nylon

Getting Started!

As someone new to the sport, you would be wise to focus on incorporating each activity into your training schedule one at a time. Most advise to begin with swimming, as this will take the longest time to develop and may also benefit from technical coaching (see the section on wild swimming). Then, you can move on to cycling and finally on to running. If you just want to give triathlon a try for the fun of it, there's no need to invest in a trisuit, because you can wear an ordinary swimsuit and change into clothes during the first transition instead. Whilst you're unlikely to find a local triathlon-specific club to join, you may find it helpful to go along to a swim, cycle and/or running club as part of your training schedule.

Support Recommendations

It is very important that you use the same kit during a race that you have been training in, otherwise you might find yourself uncomfortable or even in pain on the day from new kit. To choose which triathlon event to participate in, definitely consider the time of year it is being held at and the size of audience that it is likely to draw. Don't aim for a summer triathlon if you struggle with the heat, and don't turn up at the most popular event on the race calendar if crowds make you nervous! Finally, if the race that you are entering offers a pre-start orientation session, make sure that you arrive early enough to go to it. These sessions are invaluable for familiarizing yourself with the course, understanding the rules of what you can take with you and getting to know where the entry and exit points of the transition areas are.

PROFILE
Name: Sam Holness
Country: England
Activity: Triathlon

How did you first get started with triathlon?
Before I started triathlon, I was doing 5km park runs and then moved up to 10km runs. In 2015 I did my first duathlon, which is a run–bike–run race. Basically, it is a triathlon without the swim. I did

Photo credit: Sportograf

my first triathlon in 2016 at Dorney Lake, where the UK 2012 Olympics rowing events took place. I did a sprint triathlon race to start with. I was apprehensive and anxious because of the crowds and the noise. These are two things that were stressful to me because of my autism. So I sang 'Hakuna Matata' from *The Lion King*, to help shut out everything around me and make me feel calmer.

What are the benefits that you have found from participating in triathlon?

My parents were important in my decision to become a triathlete. My dad found some research that identified that people with autism have a life expectancy of 54 years. That's 18 years less than their neurotypical peers in the UK. Because my parents wanted to ensure that I have a long and healthy life, they encouraged me to take up sport and healthy eating. The best things about participating in triathlons are the training, racing and getting a medal at the end. I like training because it is structured and repetitive, racing because I get to travel to some interesting places and medals – well, I just like medals, haha!

What are the main sensory issues, if any, that you face whilst taking part in a triathlon?

There are so many sensory issues that I need to manage. There are the crowds, the noise and being unfamiliar with new surroundings. I am not afraid of swimming because I could swim at three years old, but learning to run and ride a bike was difficult because I had very weak motor skills (that have become much better with training). Aside from the sensory issues, I also have irritable bowel syndrome – very common amongst people with autism – which means that I need to know where the closest toilet is during a race, so that I can get there quickly if I need to.

How has being autistic impacted you (positively and/or negatively) in this activity?

Being autistic has been very positive for me. I hope that doing triathlons continues to raise the awareness of autism and motivates those on the spectrum to become healthier. I have also had a lot of publicity in magazines, on social media and on TV. However, having an invisible disability means that most people don't know that I am autistic until they interact with me. Overall, it has been very positive, and I like seeing my picture and reading stories about me in the press.

What advice would you give to an autistic young person who is interested in starting triathlon?

My first piece of advice is to learn to swim. I would also suggest taking as much time as you need before attempting your first race – don't start with an Ironman. Because of my autism, it takes me much longer to learn things, but the good news is that I never give up and keep trying until I can master a task. So, get out there and start exercising. If you can't run, start by walking. Being a triathlete will make you feel healthier, happier and help you to live longer. It is a wonderful sport to participate in.

WILD SWIMMING

Introduction

Once upon a time, wild swimming was the only kind of swimming that we humans did. Before leisure centres with pools there were rivers, lakes and the sea. The good news is, those are all still there for you to enjoy, ideally on a warm summer's day, with a picnic for afterwards. Something I learned from my research that fascinates me is that, with the exception of proboscis monkeys, humans are the only member of the primate family who find joy in playing in water regularly. Our children even take to water naturally from birth, unlike other primate species.

Why Try It?

Unless you live in a tropical climate, the places that you are going to be wild swimming will feel cold against your skin. Don't let this put you off, though, as cold water swimming is known to provide a number of health benefits, from boosting your immune system to relaxing the mind to delivering a natural endorphin kick. (Endorphins are the 'feel-good' chemicals produced by our brains!) Much like snorkelling in the ocean or sea, wild swimming in a local lake or river is going to give you a whole new perspective on the natural environment and the ecosystems that thrive there.

Sensory Expectations

Being cold is going to have a big impact on your experience of being in the water, so remember that it will take a few minutes from first immersion for you to begin feeling comfortable with the temperature. Your swimming ability will be reduced, which means that the way your body moves in a lake or river will feel differently than when you learned to swim in a pool. Never let yourself get to the point of shivering, as this is a dangerous sign. If you start to experience shivers, make your way back onto the shore as quickly as it is safe to do so, and start warming yourself up with a towel or dry robe.

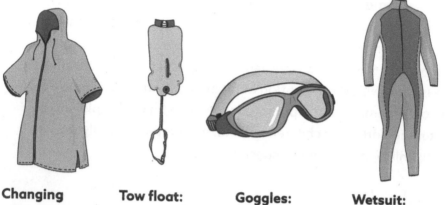

Changing robe: nylon outer shell with polyester lining

Tow float: nylon

Goggles: plastic frame with silicone strap

Wetsuit: neoprene

Getting Started!

As well as a towel or changing robe, you'll also need a swimsuit or wetsuit and a bag to take your wet kit home with you afterwards. Old trainers or a similar type of shoe are a great option to wear if you want to feel a bit more confident in the water, as you don't have to worry about accidentally standing on something unpleasant. The places to avoid when choosing your first spot to try this activity out are urban rivers, canals, flood plains or anywhere near people who are fishing. Feeling like a mermaid isn't quite so cool when it's because you're caught in someone's net! Instead, go for places that have good access via a footpath or footbridge, ideally a river or lake beach that has a gradual slope into the water. You should know what I'm going to say next by now – always make sure to let a parent or guardian know what your plans are and who you are going with. Anyone trying this activity must be a strong swimmer already.

Support Recommendations

The golden rule of wild swimming is this: always figure out how you will exit the water before you enter it. There surely could be nothing worse than launching yourself into the river with an excited holler, only to realize you're stuck in there until someone rescues you because the banks are all too steep to climb. It's recommended that this activity is done in pairs or small groups, as this means there's always somebody around to help if you need it. Help doesn't just need to come from other people, however; if you struggle with maintaining your balance whilst floating, don't feel like you can't take an inflatable with you. You most definitely can!

WHERE IN THE WORLD?

If I suggested it would be fun to swim 29km across the Palk Strait, a sea channel connecting Sri Lanka and India, what would your response be? To tell me I'm a bit mad, maybe? Well, in March 2022 13-year-old autistic swimmer Jiya Rai did just that, in 13 hours and 10 minutes. What makes this achievement even more impressive (and it already was VERY impressive!) is that Jiya had to contend with high winds at the start of her swim due to a cyclone brewing in the nearby Andaman Islands. Fortunately, her safety was secured by the escort of both the Sri Lankan and Indian Navy and Coast Guard in their respective waters. Now, Jiya has her sights set on even bigger goals: to swim the seven seas (Arctic, North Atlantic, South Atlantic, North Pacific, South Pacific, Indian and Southern). I can't wait to see it!

ALLIE'S AUTISTIC AND ADVENTUROUS MANIFESTO

You've made it to the end! That's an achievement in and of itself, so I'd now consider your first step towards becoming an adventurer complete. I'm glad that you decided to come along on this journey with me and that you chose to learn more about all of the awesome active pursuits that are out there to get involved with. This time of your life is perfect for trying out a new sport or activity, especially as schools and colleges often have so many things that you can take part in. I didn't make the most of that when I was your age, so I'd recommend not repeating my mistake!

If it's alright with you, I'm going to leave you with something to think about, and a manifesto to live by.

If you're old enough to be on social media, or you've maybe watched a few extreme sport documentaries like me, you might have noticed that a lot of these athletes are hyped up for tackling their adventures 'unsupported'. I get that this happens for a reason, but I'm here to argue that it's not particularly healthy, or indeed helpful. When people proudly declare that they are taking on some seemingly insurmountable challenge unsupported, without backup, without the help of others or aids, they're sending out a message (whether they intend to or not). And that message is: *if you need support to achieve something, that achievement is somehow worth less than theirs.*

And that is simply not true.

I hope that by reading this book you have realized that you are capable of wondrous things. Maybe even things that you thought autistic people just didn't do. I hope that you have read these words and understood that needing support is not and will never be a sign of weakness. Rather, it is a sign of self-awareness, that you know yourself well enough to say: *this is what I want to do and this is what it will take for me to get there.*

So that's the something for you to think about. Now, we get to the manifesto to live by. To every person who buys, borrows, reads or talks about this book – THANK YOU. You are now part of something bigger, a global conversation, the building of a community of autistic young people who belong in the great outdoors just as much as anybody else. If that sounds like a movement that matters to you, then take a look at the manifesto on the next page. I think it'll be right up your street.

BEING AUTISTIC AND ADVENTUROUS MEANS...

- ## Trying the thing
  Walt Disney once said, 'all our dreams can come true, if we have the courage to pursue them'. So, whatever it is you're dreaming of, just try it! Choose to be courageous and have a go, even when you're not sure you can do it. You'll never know unless you try.

- ## Asking for support
  Always remember what we talked about earlier – asking for support is not a sign of weakness. It's about you setting your sights on a goal and making sure that you have all the right things in place to get there and achieve it.

- ## Respecting your limits
  Throughout this book I've emphasized that, if you start feeling overwhelmed or unhappy, it's time to stop whatever it is you're doing. It's okay to come back and try again another day. Your wellbeing is always the most important thing.

- ## Being an adventurer
  Adventure isn't just something you do; it's part of who you are. Choosing to be an adventurer means choosing to see the possibilities for adventure in every aspect of your life! Start looking at the world around you through this lens, and you might just be surprised by what you find there.

INDEX

* Categorizable under multiple types.